文物上的楚文化

刘芬　编著

CHU CULTURE IN RELICS

WUHAN UNIVERSITY PRESS
武汉大学出版社

图书在版编目(CIP)数据

文物上的楚文化/刘芬编著.—武汉：武汉大学出版社，2019.10
ISBN 978-7-307-21160-5

Ⅰ.文…　Ⅱ.刘…　Ⅲ.楚文化—文化传播—研究—中国
Ⅳ.K871.34

中国版本图书馆 CIP 数据核字(2019)第 203935 号

责任编辑:谢群英　　责任校对:李孟潇　　版式设计:马　佳

出版发行：**武汉大学出版社**　（430072　武昌　珞珈山）
（电子邮箱：cbs22@whu.edu.cn　网址：www.wdp.whu.edu.cn）
印刷：北京虎彩文化传播有限公司
开本:720×1000　1/16　印张:9　字数:128 千字　插页:1
版次:2019 年 10 月第 1 版　2019 年 10 月第 1 次印刷
ISBN 978-7-307-21160-5　定价:29.00 元

前　言

楚文化因楚国和楚人而得名，它既是周代荆楚地域的主体文化，又是秦汉以后荆楚文化的源头。

楚文化的历史遗存埋没在地底下达两三千年之久，直到20世纪20至40年代才被盗墓者惊起，出土了战国时期的许多楚文物，其中不少青铜器和漆器工艺精妙、风格独特，让史学家和古董商惊叹不已。从20世纪50年代起，楚文化的遗存一批又一批地被考古学家唤醒，给文化界带来一阵又一阵狂喜——

1957年在河南信阳1号楚墓出土的编钟，演奏的乐曲音色、音质十分优美，我国第一颗人造卫星上演奏的《东方红》乐曲，就是由这套编钟演奏的。1957年安徽省寿县城东丘家花园出土战国时期鄂君启铜节。1965年12月，湖北荆州江陵望山楚墓出土举世闻名的越王勾践剑。1973年湖北大冶发掘铜绿山古矿冶遗址。1978年，河南淅川下寺楚墓中出土王子午升鼎、云纹铜禁。1978年湖北随州出土曾侯乙编钟、青铜尊盘。1983年在湖北省江陵县马山楚墓出土吴王夫差矛。1978年荆州天星观1号楚墓出土迄今为止最精美的虎座凤鸟漆木架鼓。1982年湖北江陵马山1号楚墓出土大量战国丝织品和刺绣品。1987年湖北荆门包山2号楚墓出土战国楚简。1993年湖北省荆门郭店村郭店一号楚墓发掘出竹简804枚。1979年到2001年，荆州博物馆的考古工作者在楚国故都纪南城遗址西北，发现目前国内所见规模最大、保存最好、陵园分布最完整的楚国高等级贵族墓地——熊家冢楚墓，于是中国文物考古界有了“北有兵马俑，南有熊家冢”之说……

就在本书校稿期间，国家文物局8月6日召开的“考古中国”重大项目新进展工作会上公布：湖北省随州市枣树林共发现了春秋墓葬55座、马坑3座、车坑4座，出土青铜器千余件，是曾国考古乃至两周考古的又一重大发现，填补了春秋中期曾国考古的空白。另外，新发现两组曾侯夫妇合葬墓，即“曾侯求”及其夫人“渔”墓、“曾侯宝”及其夫人“随仲芈加”墓。这次考古发现最让人震动的是，芈加墓出土19件编钟上的铭文，竟然是以墓主人芈加自己的口吻，讲述了曾国的历史和自己的历史。

惊起却回首。楚国八百年，从熊绎筚路蓝缕、辟在荆山，到楚庄王饮马黄河、问鼎中原；从熊渠将长江中游的铜矿纳入囊中，到秦将白起拔起郢都；从吴起变法，到屈原新政；从庄子鼓盆而歌到屈子行吟侧畔……俱往矣，风烟俱净，但遗迹犹存。荆楚大地，物华天宝，果真像辛弃疾所感慨过的：“千古江山，英雄无觅孙仲谋处。舞榭歌台，风流总被雨打风吹去。斜阳草树，寻常巷陌，人道寄奴曾住。”

楚学泰斗张正明先生曾评价丝织刺绣、青铜冶铸与髹漆工艺为“楚国物质文化的三大支柱”；楚文化专家王生铁先生将楚文化概括为“六大支柱”和“五大精神”，这六大支柱包括炉火纯青的青铜冶炼铸造、绚丽精美的丝织刺绣、巧夺天工的木竹漆器、义理精深的老庄哲学、惊才绝艳的屈骚文学和诙谐鬼怪的美术乐舞；五大精神则是筚路蓝缕的艰苦创业精神、追新逐异的开拓进取精神、兼收并蓄的开放融会精神、崇武卫疆的强军爱国精神以及重诺贵和的诚信和谐精神。

“文物是文化的载体，是一种物化了的文化。”在“博物馆热”持续走红的今天，越来越多的人开始“为一个馆，赴一座城”。今天的博物馆也不再是冷冰冰的文物陈列室，而是渐渐成为现代科技与文化积淀共存的网红地标，但如何“活化”文物，如何挖掘文物背后的历史文化，透过文物，“见事、见人、见精神”，依然是博物馆、文化工作者、教育工作者需要思考和努力的问题。

八百年荆楚历史文化遗存，灿若星河。作为一个生活在荆楚大地的现代人，笔者只能是凭借一个博物馆志愿者的热心和一个教育工作者的热诚，像一个导游一样，把自己无数次凝望星空时看到的几颗耀眼的星光指出来，给你看——

朋友，荆楚大地，人杰地灵，物华天宝。慢慢走，欣赏啊！

Contents

Chapter 1

Chu Culture in Relics

1.1 Intruduction to Chu Culture

Chu Culture, named after the State of Chu and the people of Chu State, is both the subjective culture in the area of Jing and Chu in the Zhou Dynasty and the source of Jing-Chu Culture in the following Qin and Han dynasties.

The Gate of Chu Town (Mountain Moshan of the East Lake, Wuhan)

The entrance to the Chu Cultural Tourist Area was designed in 1992 according to the city gate of Jinancheng, the capital city of Chu State in the Warring States Period. It consists of the water gate, the land gate, the wall, the watch tower, the arrow tower and the beacon tower. Since the Chu custom valued the color red, the wall was built with the red sandstone from Daye, the ancient copper mine site in Chu State. Above the gate, there was the title of "Chu Cheng" in oracle by the famous historian Hu Houxuan.

According to Zhang Zhengming① Chu Culture can be divided into 5 periods, that is, the original period, the growing period, the prosperous period, the sluggish period, and the transformation period.

In the Spring and Autumn Period, the culture in Jing-Chu area developed their own characteristics with six pillars② such as advanced bronze smelting and casting technology, delicately embroidered silk, colorful painted lacquers, unique philosophy of Laozi and Zhuangzi, novel literature of Quyuan, and arresting music and dance. These present a picture of a sophisticated society in the southern Chu State rivaling the grandest principalities in the north③.

The Tablet of "Chu Tian Zhu Feng" (Mountain Moshan of the East Lake, Wuhan)④

① 张正明在《楚文化史》中将楚文化发展历程分为五个时期：滥觞期、茁长期、鼎盛期、滞缓期和转化期。

② 春秋战国时期，荆楚地区的文化发展走上了一条个性化发展的道路，青铜冶铸技术高度发展，丝织刺绣技术后来居上，木竹漆器流光溢彩，老庄哲学独树一帜，屈骚文学"别创新体"，美术乐舞动人心魄。这是楚文化的六大支柱。

③ 王生铁，《楚文化概要》，湖北人民出版社，2013。

④ 楚城"楚天翥风"牌匾题字。风为传说中的神鸟，翥有高飞之意。牌匾意为凤凰在楚国的天空中展翅高飞。凤翥出自晋·陆机《浮云赋》："鸾翔凤翥，鸿惊鹤飞，鲸鲵溯波，鲛鳄冲道。"

The Phoenixes Emblem in Mountain Moshan of the East Lake

Chu Tian Terrace①

① 楚天台的建筑造型是根据古代楚国的"章华台"设计的，层台累榭，钟鼓楚韵，外五内六层，是武汉东湖的地标性建筑。

The famous historian Mr. Fan Wenlan once pointed out: "The expansion of Chu State for more than 800 years has provided important conditions for the establishment of the great feudal empire in Qin and Han. Among the seven states, the Chu and Qin had made more contribution to history." ①

Ancient Chinese Script "Chu" (after Chinese Inscription Dictionary)

Xu Shen in the Han Dynasty defined the word Chu and Jing as clusters of prickly bushes in his etymological dictionary *Shuo Wen Jie Zi* (*Origin of Chinese Characters by Xu Shen*). The early graph representing the word Chu shows a foot surrounded by vegetation while the graph represents a place name as early as 1200 BC.

The historian Gu Jigang said that it was because the Chu people built the country in the jungle, and another historian Xu Zhongshu said that it was because the Chu people planted "Jing" other than "Chu" in the village to defend themselves. In the northern countries, "Jing" and "Chu" were used interchangeably, and the Chu people usually called themselves "Chu" as well as "Jing". In the Chu bamboo slips excavated from Tomb No. 2 in Baoshan Jingmen, the Chu King was addressed as the Jing King.

① 张正明，《楚文化史》，上海人民出版社，1987，p. 1。

The Bronze Script of "Chu" in the Bo Bell of Marquis Yi of Zeng State①
(Hubei Provincial Museum)

1.2 Famous Chu Historical and Cultural Celebrities

In the process of the development of Chu State and the formation of Chu Culture, the Chu people had built their spirits which shows the connotation and essence of Chu Culture. These can be summarized into five kinds of spirits②, namely, the innovative spirit in hard work, the pioneering spirit in pursuing freshness and novelty, the opening spirit in embracing and integrating diversity, the patriotic spirit in strengthening the army and protecting the territory, and the spirit of honesty and harmony in credit and

① 湖北省博物馆藏曾侯乙镈钟上的铭文"楚"。
② 王生铁,《楚文化概要》, 湖北人民出版社, 2013。

promise①.

During the Xia and Shang dynasties, different tribes were fiercely contested in the Central Plains region, and the Zhu Rong tribe fell apart. Jilian, a Mi family-named tribe of the Zhu Rong tribe, went to the remote south (the present Jing-Chu area) for the survival and development of the tribe. The Jilian tribe integrated the culture of the Central Plains with the indigenous culture of the south and made themselves a strong tribe.

The Statue of Zhu Rong Observing Stars in Mountain Moshan, Wuhan
Zhu Rong is known as the ancestor of the Chu people, the fire god who rules the fire.

① 在楚国发展壮大和楚文化的形成过程中，楚文化的优秀内涵与卓异精髓日益凸显，可以归纳为五种精神：即筚路蓝缕的艰苦创业精神、追新逐异的开拓创新精神、兼收并蓄的开放融会精神、崇武卫疆的强军爱国精神和重诺贵和的诚信和谐精神。

The southern Jilian tribe formed a new tribe named "Jingchu" or "Chu Jing", "Chu Barbarians" or "Jing Barbarians". In the last years of the Shang Dynasty, a famous leader Yu Xiong in Chu realized that the rising Zhou clan was a force that could be relied upon and went to the leader of the Zhou family, that is, Xi Bo Jichang (King Wen of Zhou) to seek shelter. The Zhou court showed their respect to Yu Xiong and gave him the family name "Xiong", thus the later king of Chu State was named after Xiong.

The Statue of Yu Xiong①
(The Sculptures of Chu Talents, Mountain Moshan of the East Lake, Wuhan)

① 图片来自：https://www.meipian.cn/1gu33t8x

Xiong Yi, the grandchild of the fourth generation since Yu Xiong, was given the title of "Zi Nan" by King Cheng of the Zhou Dynasty, which marked the beginning of Chu State.

The Statue of Xiong Yi Guarding the Fire While Offering Sacrifice to Heaven
(The Scupture of Chu Talents)

From Xiong Yi to Xiong Qu, Chu State became more and more powerful and began to get rid of the boundary of the Zhou Dynasty and develop in its own way.

During Xiong Qu's reign, Chu State developed quickly. Xiong Qu conquered the State of Yong and expanded the land to the west (now Zhushan County, Hubei Province). Later, Xiong Qu drove away the Yang & Yue states eastward and controlled the whole Jianghan Plain. When the King of Zhou Dynasty marched to the State of E (now Ezhou, Wuhan area), Xiong

Qu seized this chance and occupied the land in the State of E. The rich copper mine in E naturally became the property of Chu State, which directly laid the foundation for the vigorous development of Chu State in the following centuries.

The Story of Xiong Qu Shooting the Stone

Han Shi Wai Zhuan recorded the story of Xiong Qu: "Once Xiong Qu walked in the evening and saw a big stone in the darkness. He mistook it as a tiger lying on the ground and shot it. The feather of the arrow was lost. The subordinates went to check the target and found it a big stone." ① Xiong Qu, together with Hou Yi and Yang Youji, was regarded as the most famous archers in Chinese legends.

During the period of King Wu, King Wen, King Cheng, and King Mu, the State of Chu wiped out many small states in the neighborhood and cleared up the way to the Central Plain.

① 《韩诗外传》:"昔者楚熊渠子夜行，寝石，以为伏虎，弯弓而射之，没金饮羽。下视，知其为石。"

The Statue of King Wu of Chu and His Wife Deng Man①

① 邓曼，春秋时邓国的公族之女，楚武王的夫人，楚文王的母亲。邓曼为人贤惠聪颖，常对楚武王的某些活动进行商讨和谋划。邓曼被后人认为是“知人”“知天道”的贤内助。

The Statue of King Wen of Chu

The Statue of King Zhuang of Chu

King Zhuang ascended throne in 613 BC when he was about 20 years old. At that time, the political power in Chu State was corrupt and the regime was extremely unstable. In this situation, King Zhuang presided over the political affairs very cautiously, so there came the famous allusion of "Startling the world with a single cry"①. Later, King Zhuang carried out a series of reforms in political, economic and military and laid the foundation for the hegemony of Chu. In 606 BC, King Zhuang marched northward and quested power in the Central Plains, and Chu State entered its heyday.

After King Zhuang, the national strength of Chu State was gradually weakening because of the battle with Jin and Wu. In the time of King Zhao and King Hui, Chu recovered and regained its strength and became one of the

① 朱一飞、佘长茂、王海燕编著，《中国文化寓言故事》，上海外语教育出版社，2007，p. 115。

Seven Powers of the Warring States Period. There underwent a series of ups and downs in the following generations of Kings Jian, Sheng, and Dao until King Wei made Chu State a land with the widest territory, the largest population and the strongest military strength. But in the reign of King Huai, King Huai believed in the rumor and exiled Qu Yuan, which led to the civil disorder. Chu was threatened by Qin and lost vast land to Qin. Eventually King Huai was imprisoned in the State of Qin. The State of Chu was falling.

The Statue of King Huai

In 278 BC, Bai Qi, the general of Qin State, led the troops to attack Ying, the capital of Chu. After the fall of the capital, Chu State moved the capital to Chen (present Huaiyang, Henan). In 241 BC, King Kaolie of Chu State moved the capital to Shouchun (present Shou County, Anhui Province), and the power of Chu declined gradually. In 223 BC, Wang Jian, the general of Qin State, led the army to attack the Chu Capital Shouchun. The legendary Chu State bid farewell to the stage of history.

In the history of Chu State, there are some famous district magistrates① such as Zi Wen in King Cheng's reign, Sun Shuao in King Zhuang's reign, Ye Gong in King Zhao's reign and Huang Xie in King Qingxiang and King Kaolie's reigns. They assisted the kings in governing the state and made their own contribution to the economic, political and cultural development of Chu. Their wisdom and effort have had far-reaching influences on later generations.

The Statue of Four Famous Ministers in Chu State②
From left to right: Zi Wen, Sun Shuao, Ye Gong, Huang Xie

① 令尹是楚国在春秋战国时代的最高官衔，是掌握政治事务、发号施令的最高官，对内主持国事，对外主持战争，总揽军政大权于一身。令尹主要由楚国贵族当中的贤能来担任。

② 楚国历史上的四大令尹：楚成王时的子文，被孔子誉为“忠”；孙叔敖，楚庄王时任十三年令尹，辅助庄王成就霸业，治水功绩名垂千古；楚昭王时的叶公，善于治水而好龙；黄歇，也就是春申君，在白起拨郢之后帮助楚倾襄王和楚考烈王复兴楚国。

The Statue of Sun Shuao Taming Water

The Statue of Qu Yuan

The Statue of King Zhao Interviewing Confucius

The Statue of Zhuangzi and *A Happy Excursion*

The Statue of Yu Boya①

---

① 俞伯牙，春秋战国时期楚国郢都(今湖北荆州)人，任职晋国上大夫，精通琴艺。伯牙抚琴遇知音就是他在回楚国途中发生的故事。

The Monument of *Li Sao*

With a height of 14. 8 meters and a base width of 17 meters, Li Sao Monument is one of the largest steles with inscriptions in China.

Li Sao is Qu Yuan's masterpiece in the history of Chinese literature. The total poem consists of 2, 490 words in 373 sentences. The poem is the reproduction of Mao Zedong's handwriting of "Li Sao" in Wei Style when he was studying in Hunan First Normal School in 1913.

Chapter 2

Chu Mythology in Lacquered Wares

In ancient times, the southern Chu State was a mysterious world. Many myths and legends were circulated and integrated here: Shennong, Jingwei, Gonggong, Xingtian, Kuafu and other mythical gods or heroes all embodied the spirit and belief on this land. At the same time, it was also the world of witchcrafts, where people lived with deities and shamans.

2.1 Zhu Rong, the God of Fire

Each tribe or nation has its own ancient ancestor, a deified person or a personified god, who gives the nation courage and faith and is worshiped by the people. There is some documental and archaeological evident that Zhu Rong, the Fire God, was the earliest ancestor of the Chu people.

In *Zuo Zhuan* there recorded that Kuizi, the lord of Chu State conferred in another region, did not offer sacrifice to Zhu Rong and Yu Xiong. The Chu King was so angry with it that he dismissed Kuizi and eliminated his land. Since Yu Xiong was the far ancestor of the first king of Chu State and Zhu Rong was the forefather of the Chu people, it was unforgivable for Kuizi not to offer sacrifice to Yu Xiong and Zhu Rong.

The bamboo slips unearthed from the Tomb No. 2 in Baoshan Jingmen in

Hubei Province in 1987, which is the newest archaeological evidence of Zhu Rong as the earliest ancestor of the Chu people. recorded the names of the ancestors of the tomb owner. Zhu Rong was among them. Although "Lao Tong" was older than Zhu Rong and was recorded in these bamboo slips, "Lao Tong" was not worshiped as the earliest ancestor since he had not made great achievements for the later generations.

How did Zhu Rong look like? *Shan Hai Jing* (*The Classics of Mountains and Seas*), which was the collection of witchcrafts in the Warring States Period, recorded different images of Zhu Rong. In *Shan Hai Jing*, *Hai Wai Nan Jing*, Zhu Rong was described as "Zhu Rong lived in the south. He had the beast's body, man's face, and drived two dragons."

The Heroic Deeds of Zhu Rong

Huo Zheng (Fire Corrector) in the legendary period was addressed as "Huo Shi" (Fire Master) in the Zhou Dynasty. The duties of the fire master include the following: one is to observe the astrology and announce the farming season, another is to set fire on the uncultivated land, and the third is to keep the fire while offering sacrifice to heaven.

2.1.1 To Observe the Astrology and Announce the Farming Season

Farming season decides the agricultural activities. Plant in Spring, grow in Summer, harvest in Autumn, and store in Winter. The best season for plowing and sowing in the middle reaches of the Yellow River is in the Spring Equinox. Zhu Rong was known as Huo Zheng because he could determine the date of the Spring Equinox according to when and where Mars appeared.

The Mars observed by Zhu Rong is a star known as the "Da Huo" (Big Fire, the Western Scorpio). The moment when the Mars were rising in the east was known as "Hun Jian" (Seen at Dusk). Around 2300 BC (in the Early Xia Dynasty), the moment when "Da Huo" was seen at dusk happened to be the Spring Equinox. When the Fire Corrector observed the Big Fire at dusk, he could announce the coming of the Spring Equinox①.

2.1.2 To Set Fire on the Uncultivated land

In ancient time, people cut woods with axes and burned the uncultivated land with fire. Farming began with burning the uncultivated land, which was the preface of harvest as well as a joyful ceremony.

Who would lead the fire which was kept for a winter to the field and set the fire on the uncultivated land? It should be the Fire Corrector who set the fire on the field in Spring and kept the fire after the Mars set in the west in Autumn.

2.1.3 To Keep the Fire While Offering Sacrifice to Heaven

Li Ji recorded that "Roast meat on the altar for sacrifice" in the Zhou Dynasty. In the ceremony in the Zhou Dynasty, the sacrificial offerings would

① 张正明,《楚史》, 湖北教育出版社, 1995, pp. 8-9。

The Statue of Zhu Rong Observing Stars in Mountain Moshan, Wuhan

The Statue of Zhu Rong Observing Stars was designed and completed by Professor Xiang Jinguo of Hubei Academy of Arts in 1992. Zhu Rong is known as the ancestor of the Chu people, the fire god who rules the fire. The statue is made of cast iron with the height of 5. 5 meters and weight of 5. 6 tons. The base is 1. 5 meters high with the nine-layer circular steps which symbolize the nine layers of heavens. In this statue, Zhu Rong is gazing the sky, with his left hand holding the pictograph of "斗" from the 28 constellations unearthed from the tomb of Marquis Yi of Zeng, his right hand holding the oracle bone of the Shang Dynasty, on which there write the scripts meaning "the sun of the east gradually brightens, while the moon in the south gradually falls". This symbolizes Zhu Rong observes the movement of stars. There are fire and flame on Zhu Rong's brows, legs, and thighs, which shows Zhu Rong as a fire god. Zhu Rong squats with one foot on the sun and the other on the moon, and with angry eyes and convex belly, showing his vitality.

On the back of this statue, Zhu Rong is transformed into a divine image of a phoenix. Imitating the "three-headed phoenix" on the silk fabric unearthed from the Chu Tomb of Mashan Jiangling in Warring States Period, the designer made the head, the hairpin and the back into a great phoenix with angry eyes, agitating belly and flapping wings. In 2010, the sculpture won the "New China Urban Construction Achievement Award".

be put on the firewood to roast and the flavor of the roasted meat would go up to the sky. When the Heavenly Emperor smelt the flavor, he received the offering. In this ceremony, it was the Fire Corrector who set the fire and guarded the sacrifice.

Zhu Rong Peak of the Southern Sacred Mountain Heng in Hunan Province

In the legendary era, the Chu people lived in the middle reaches of the Yellow River and belonged to the Yandi system in culture. Because Zhu Rong was good at observing the stars and contributed a lot to the development of agriculture, he was regarded as the earliest ancestor. Zhu Rong became a full-time witch with his own knowledge of astronomy, history and witchcraft. An outstanding witch would be admired by the tribes during his lifetime, and would be deified after his death. Zhong and Li were Fire Correctors before death, the fire god after death, and were given the title of Zhu Rong, which were upgraded to the Thunder God.

Yun Zhongjun, the God of Thunder

Thunder is a symbol of vitality. In the early spring, the thunder begins to sound, and the vegetation become new. In the late autumn, the thunder disappears, and the trees and leaves are dying. From early spring to late autumn, it is an active and vigorous period for the thunder and the vegetations.

In the *Jiu Ge* of *Chu Ci*, Qu Yuan depicted Yun Zhongjun, the sound and shape of the god of the thunder. Yun Zhongjun was "Yunjun" in the bamboo slips unearthed from No. 1 Tomb of Tianxingguan Jiangling. In the spectrum of the gods in *Jiu Ge*, only the Eastern Emperor Taiyi, is superior to Yun Zhongjun, which shows that Yun Zhongjun was worshiped by the Chu people for their great contribution to agriculture.

The primitive belief of a nation is the projection of the ideal model of their mentality formed in their early experience. The character of a god descends to the character of man. People who respect the god of thunder, like the Chu people in the East, the Greeks and the Romans in the West, had a thunder-and-lightning-like character in their youthful period with exuberant pride, pioneering courage and passion for creation①.

2.2 Phoenix Worship in Lacquered Wares

Phoenix worshiped by the Chu people is the relic of the totem worship. For the Chu people, phoenix is the symbol of their ancestor Zhu Rong②.

*Bai Hu Tong*③ said: "The sun... located in the south, their Emperor

① 张正明,《楚史》,湖北教育出版社,1995, p. 18。

② 张正明,《楚史》,湖北教育出版社,1995, p. 15。

③ 《白虎通》记:"太阳……位在南方,……其帝炎帝……其神祝融……其精为鸟,离为鸾。"《白虎通》又称《白虎通义》,向来被视为东汉建初四年(79年)白虎观经学会议之资料汇编,此书不仅是经学发展中之产物,更是当时上自天子、下迄儒生之学术共识,具有保存当时经学样貌之典范价值。

Yan... their god Zhu Rong... his spirit became the bird... that bird is Luan (the phoenix)." Luan is the colorful bird—the phoenix. The Chu people worship the phoenix as their ancestor Zhu Rong. They love the phoenix just because they love their nation.

Among cultural remains of the heyday of Chu State, there were many unique wood carvings of the standing phoenix with a tiger base. Decorated with colorful patterns, the phoenix stood on a small while docile tiger with raised head and flung wings. This wood carving is a combination of strength, beauty and peculiarity, which can be regarded as a symbol of the peak period of Chu State and Chu Culture.

Flying Bird with a Tiger Base①
(Jingzhou Museum)

① 虎座飞鸟(荆州博物馆), 1978 年出土于天星观一号战国楚墓。

Flying Bird with a Tiger Base
(Jingzhou Museum)

The Chu people believed that the phoenix had a mysterious relationship with them and gave many beautiful characteristics to the phoenix. In the cultural relics of Chu State there are numerous images of the phoenix. A large number of exquisite phoenix-patterned or shaped lacquer wares were excavated in the Chu region, which makes this phoenix bird of the eastern land of ceremony and propriety well-known at home and abroad, spreading the light of China's long and splendid civilization.

Drum with Lacquered Tiger Base and Phoenix Stand of the Warring States Period①
(Jingzhou Museum)

This Drum with Lacquered Tiger Base and Phoenix Stand of the Warring States Period in Jingzhou Museum is one of the most exquisite drums ever discovered. It was unearthed in the No. 1 Tomb of Chu in Tianxing Temple in 1978. It is composed of the tigers, the phoenixes and the drum with practicality and artistry, which shows the unique and novel craftsmanship of the Chu people. This tiger-based and phoenix-stand drum is not only a ritual instrument but also a musical instrument with great artistic value in literature, music, painting, and modeling. It also fully reflects the spirit of the Chinese ancients who dared to conquer the wild beasts dauntlessly.

---

① 战国虎座鸟架鼓（荆州博物馆）。荆州博物馆展出的虎座鸟架鼓是迄今为止发现的最精美的虎座凤鸟漆木架鼓之一，出土于1978年荆州天星观1号楚墓内。虎座鸟架鼓将猛虎、祥凤和乐鼓三者融于一身，将实用性和艺术性完美结合，展示出了楚人与众不同的高超制乐工艺，在中国历史上留下了灿烂的一笔。虎座鸟架鼓是古代的一种乐器，与编钟、编磬组合使用，一般只出土于楚国贵族墓葬。虎座鸟架鼓既是礼器也是乐器，不仅具有文学价值、音乐价值，在绘画艺术、色彩造型等方面也受到现代审美艺术的推崇，同时还充分反映出了中国古人勇于征服猛兽、不畏强暴的精神。

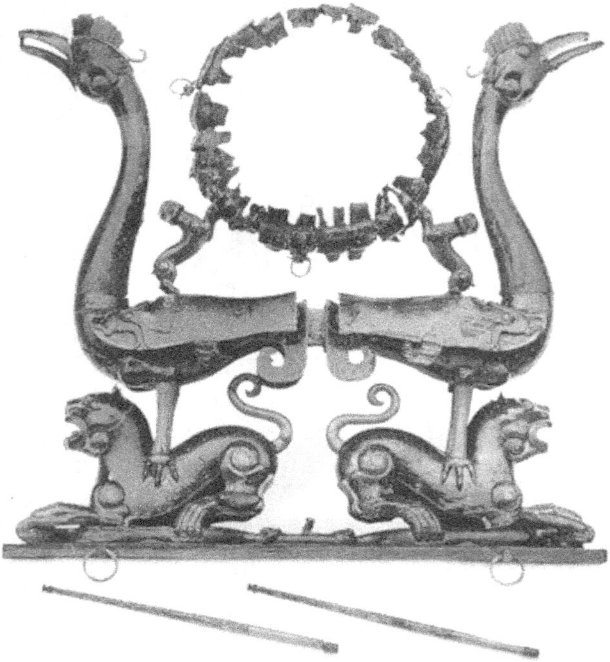

Drum with Tiger-Shaped Base and Phoenix-Shaped Stand of the Warring States Period
(Hubei Provincial Museum)

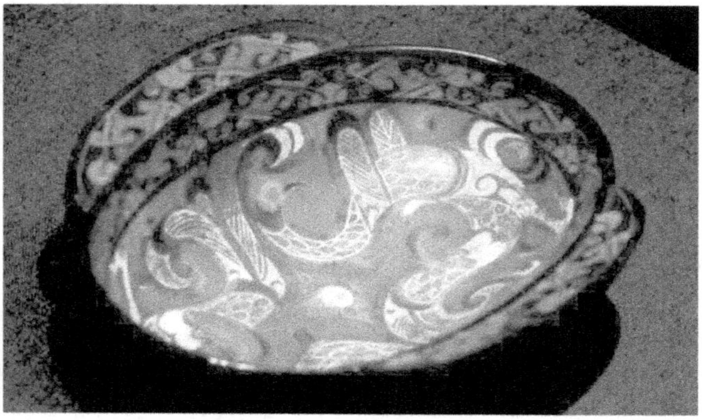

Lacquered Ear Cup with a Pair of Phoenixes
(Jingzhou Museum)

Lacquered Plate with Pattern of Singing Phoenixes and Dancing Dragons①
(Jinzhou Museum)

Double Lacquered Cup from No. 2 Baoshan Tomb of Jingmen②
(Hubei Provincial Museum)

① 彩绘龙鸟纹漆盘，1992 年湖北省江陵市高台汉墓出土。
② 战国彩绘凤鸟形双联漆杯，1987 年湖北荆门包山 2 号楚墓出土。

Lacquered Wooden Screen Unearthed from Tomb 1 at Wangshan①
(Hubei Provincial Museum)

This small lacquered wooden screen combines birds, snakes, toads, and deer in an ornamental composition. It depicts 55 animals such as phoenixes, deer, snakes and toads intertwined with each other in openwork, round carving and embossing techniques. This set of statues condensed a natural world of competition and recycling in a very limited space.

The Chu people compared themselves or others to the phoenix. For example, Qu Yuan once compared himself to the phoenix like this "The phoenix is imprisoned in the cage while the chickens and ducks are dancing"②.

There is a famous legend about King Zhuang of Chu State and the phoenix. The King Zhuang of Chu was in office for three years but he dealt with no political affairs. An official visited King Zhuang and asked him to guess a riddle. With beauties in his arms, King Zhuang interviewed that official who asked "A bird rests on Mountain Bu, having not sung or flew for three years. What kind of bird is this?" King Zhuang replied: "You haven't seen him flying for three years, once you see him fly, he must fly in the sky;

① 这件座屏以透雕、圆雕和浮雕相结合的手法，刻画出凤、鹿、蛇、蛙等55只形态各异的动物，各类动物形象相互穿插交织在一起。屏面以双凤争蛇造型为中心，左右雕刻双鹿和朱雀衔蛇，屏框旁各有凤鸟啄食蟒蛇图案，屏座由盘绕纠结的蟒与蛇组成。这组雕像在极为有限的屏面空间内，高度浓缩了自然界万类相竞、生生不息的壮观场面。

② 屈原《九章·怀沙》："凤皇在笯兮，鸡鹜翔舞。"

you haven't heard his singing for three years, once he sings, his song must shake the world."①

Lacquered Bird-man Figure Standing on the Head of a Phoenix on a Toad Base②
(Jingzhou Museum)

The lacquered statue "Yu Ren" (Feathered Man), unearthed from the No. 2 Tomb of Tianxing Temple in Jingzhou in 2000, is the treasure of Jingzhou Museum. This unique statue consists of a man with a tail and claws of the bird in the upper part, a phoenix in the middle, and a toad at the bottom as the base. This "angel" is rather a god than a human being, a testimony to the ancient witchcraft culture in Chu State.

The mythical bird (phoenix) in the sun is the transformation of the Sun God. Since the sun and the fire is red, the phoenix admired by the Chu people has the color of red. Therefore, the Chu people valued the color red③.

---

① "三年不飞，一飞冲天；三年不鸣，一鸣惊人。"

② 漆凤鸟羽人是楚国巫风最盛时代最具创意的木雕作品。它长着人的身形，却有着鸟的尾巴和爪子，腿上还依稀可以分辨出羽毛的麟状。他站在一只凤鸟的头顶，立在蟾蜍底座之上，造型十分怪异奇特。羽人被当作天上的神灵，蟾蜍代表月亮之精，凤鸟是飞翔于天地之间的神鸟，羽人又是变幻莫测的神人，三者合而为一，寄托楚人遨游九天、生命永恒的愿望。

③ 张正明，《楚史》，湖北教育出版社，1995，p. 17。

The Chu people believed that only led by the phoenix could the soul ascend the heaven and travel the universe after death. Qu Yuan described this in *Li Sao* like: "In the early morning, I set off from the ferry of the Heaven River, and in the evening I arrived at the farthest west. Take the phoenixes whose wings are like flags, and fly high in the sky like the phoenix."①

Silk Painting Depicting a Lady, Phoenix and Dragon②
(Hunan Provincial Museum)

① "朝发轫于天津兮，夕余至乎西极。凤皇翼其承旗兮，高翱翔之翼翼。"

② 长沙陈家大山楚墓出土帛画《人物龙凤图》，又称《龙凤仕女图》，1949 年出土于湖南省长沙市东南郊楚墓，是现存最早的中国帛画之一，也是中华人民共和国 2002 年公布的 64 件禁止出国(境)展览文物之一。是中国战国中晚期的帛画精品，画中绘有龙凤和着云纹广袖绣衣长裙、高髻的贵族妇女。现藏于湖南省博物馆。

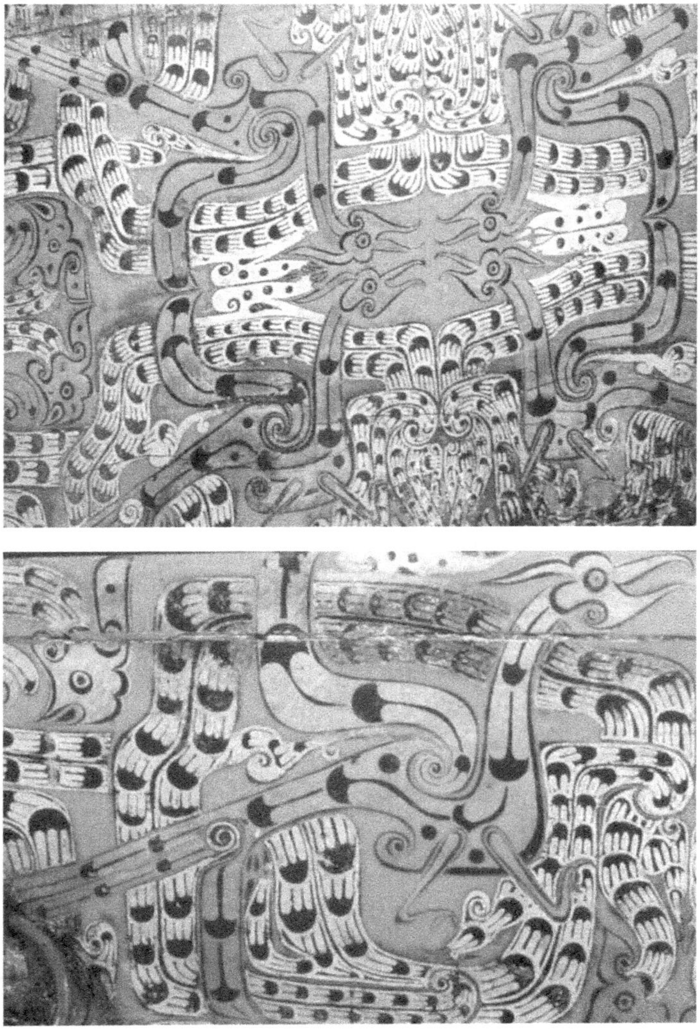

Part of the Color-lacquered Inner Coffin①
(Unearthed at No. 2 Tomb of Baoshan, Jingmen, Hubei Province)

On the panel of this inner coffin, the dragon and the phoenix are the theme of painting, while the phoenix pattern is in a dominant position and the dragon pattern overlaps the phoenix pattern, which shows the worship of the phoenix for the Chu people.

---

① 战国楚国彩漆龙凤纹内棺局部。1987 年湖北荆门包山 2 号墓出土。彩绘内棺中龙凤是彩绘主题，凤纹居于主导地位，龙纹交叠于凤纹之下，楚人崇凤，可见一斑。

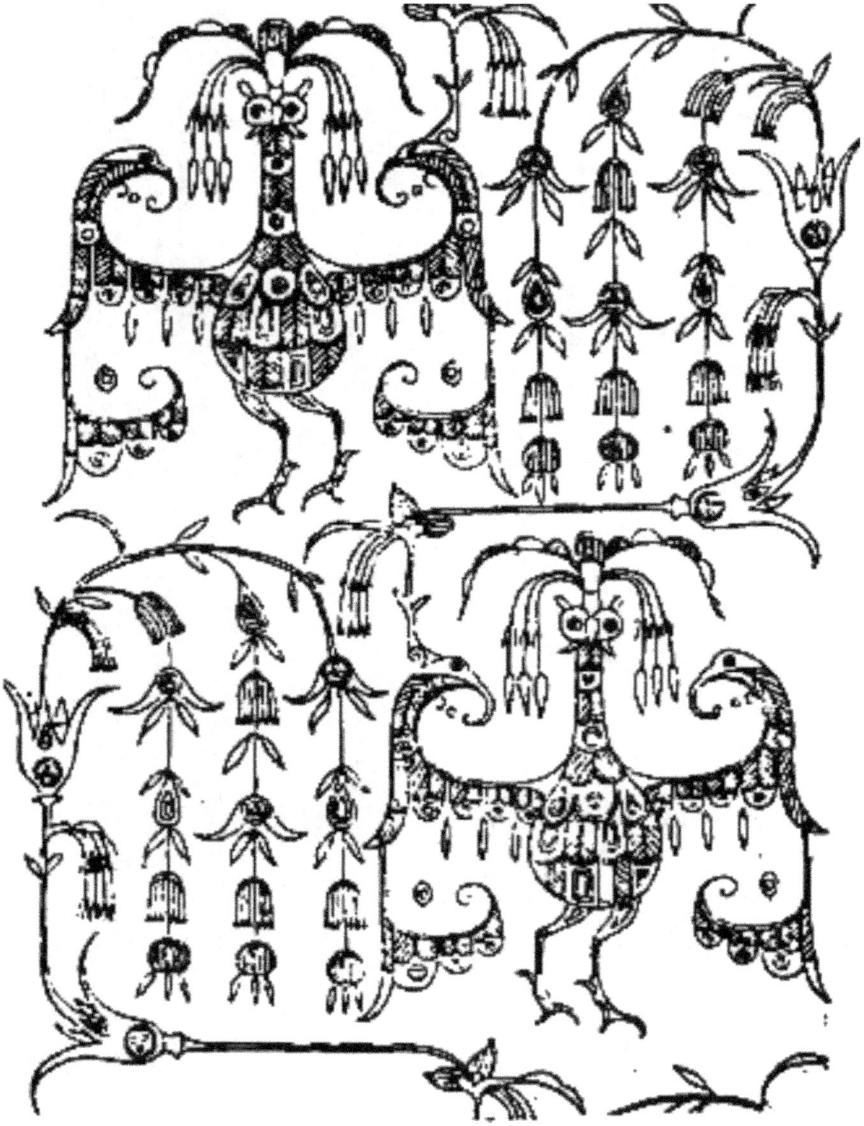

Embroidered Silk with Pattern of Phoenixes from No. 1 Tomb at Mashan Jiangling①
(Jinzhou Museum)

① 三头凤刺绣，湖北江陵马山一号楚墓出土，荆州博物馆藏。

The Western Phoenix looks like an eagle with red and golden feathers. It burns itself at the age of 500 and regenerates from the ashes, which is entrusted with people's pursuit of eternality. The Chinese phoenix does not have the power of regeneration from its own ash, but it can make the world peaceful. Therefore, in Chinese culture, the phoenix entrusts people's yearning for a peaceful world. As a symbol of auspiciousness, the phoenix has been derived the meanings of beauty, nobleness and rareness. Idioms such as "Long Feng Cheng Xiang" (Dragon and phoenix are an auspicious marriage), "Feng Mao Ling Jiao" (as rare as the feather of the phoenix and the horn of a kirin) and "Feng Cai Luan Zhang" (as beautiful as the colors and patterns of a phoenix) are all derived from the phoenix. The colorful patterns of the phoenix have become a symbol of the Chu Culture, bringing people a poetic association with a mythical and magnificent world.

2.3 Other Deity Worship for the Chu People

"The Jing people respect ghosts" — The people of Chu "believed in witches and ghosts, and valued offering sacrifice to the ghosts"①. These primitive religions and witchcraft concepts dominated by ancestors and ghosts worship are embodied in the lacquer wares, which reflect the wishes and norms of the Chu people. The Chu people lived with a pantheon that ranged from local animists deities to powerful high gods.

Thousands of lacquered wares were excavated in the former territory of Chu State. There are phoenix-like birds with felines on the drum-stands, the

① 《淮南子·人间》曰："荆人畏鬼"；《汉书·地理志下》记载楚地之民"信巫鬼，重淫祀"。

torso of a creature with large eyes, protruding tongue, and long antlers, lacquered wooden screen with bird, snake, and deer in an ornamental composition, an egg-shaped box with intertwining snakes. These images with those on Marquis Yi's coffin and the Sackler manuscript suggest their popularity was deeply rooted in Chu mythology.

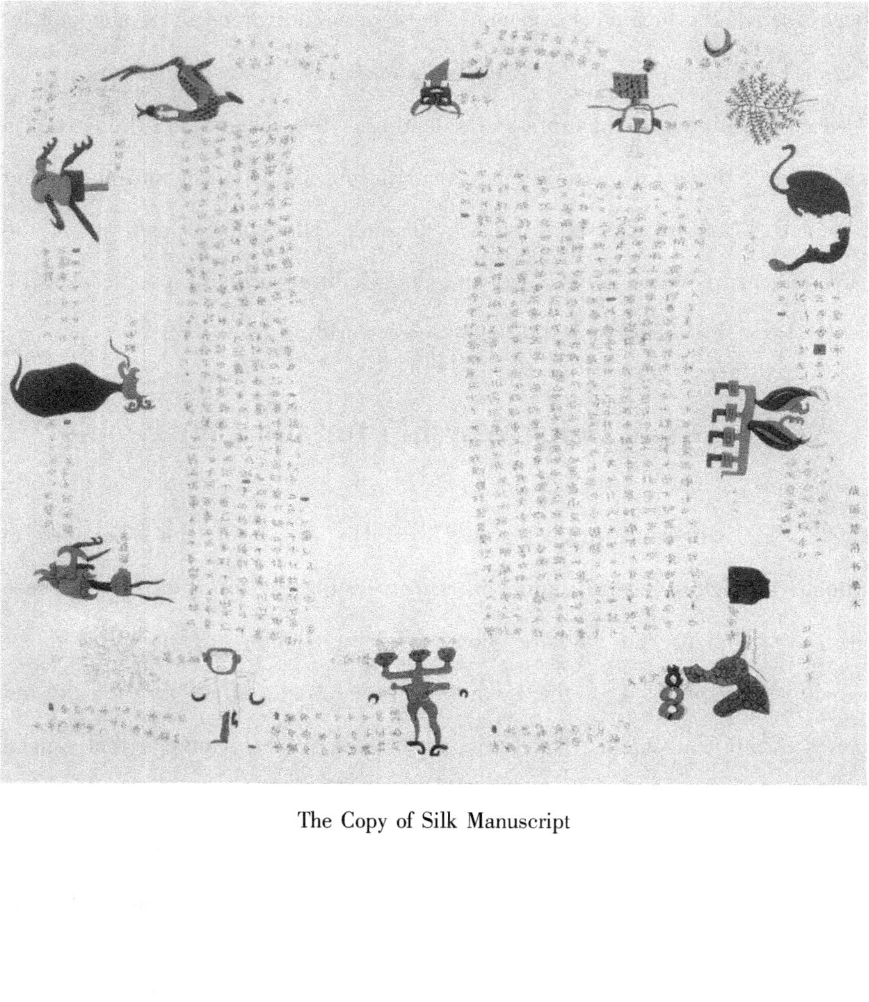

The Copy of Silk Manuscript

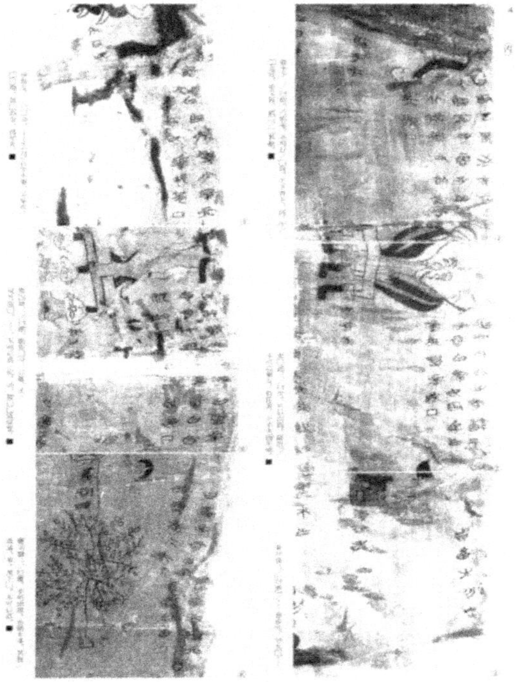

The Silk Manuscript of Chu State from Zidanku, Changsha①
(Courtesy of Arthur M. Sackler Collection, the Metropolitan Museum of Art, USA)

The text of this document is divided into two sections. The first describes the natural order and Chu's beliefs on the origins of the universe and their ancestors. The second focuses on the human order and the consequences of man's behavior in relation to Nature. Surrounding the text are twelve images depicting the gods of twelve months. At the corners are plants motifs symbolic of the four seasons. This manuscript is the earliest surviving document where ancient Chu's beliefs are recorded in writing, and illustrated systematically by a set of deities associated with the cosmic scheme.

---

① 《长沙子弹库战国楚帛书》(局部)，现收藏于美国纽约大都会艺术博物馆(The Metropolitan Museum of Art)。楚帛书，通常也叫楚缯书或楚绢书，于中华人民共和国成立前在湖南长沙东南郊子弹库战国楚墓盗掘出土，是目前出土最早的古代帛书，对研究战国楚文字以及当时的思想文化有重要参考价值。楚帛书上下高38.5厘米，左右宽46.2厘米，中心是书写方向互相颠倒的两段文字，四周是作旋转状排列的12段边文，其中每三段居于一方，四方交角用青、赤、白、黑四树相隔，每段各附有一种神怪图形。全篇共有900多字。边文12章，每章代表一个月份，各月都附有一种神怪图形。春秋战国前，湖湘地区的土著蛮越民族，大多信奉原始宗教，崇拜各种祖先之神和自然之神。楚人南下后，带来了楚人的宗教信仰、神话传说。这两种原始宗教、神话互相影响，融合在一起，构成了春秋战国时期湖南地区具有特色的宗教和神话，在长沙子弹库出土的楚帛书中得到了充分印证。

The Lacquered Wooden Tomb Guardian Figure of the Warring States Period①
(Hubei Provincial Museum)

Lacquered wooden tomb guardian is composed of long antlers, protruding tongues, and large eyes, which represented the magical power to protect the dead.

Chu artisans made these lacquered wooden sculptures for burial in a tomb. As a guardian figure it is powerful, since it combines the real and imaginary. Lacquered antlers bestow the alertness of a stag. The human face

① 战国木雕双头镇墓兽，湖北省博物馆藏。整体由底座、兽头和两对鹿角构成。背向的两只兽头曲颈相连，雕成变形龙面，巨眼圆睁，长舌至颈。镇墓兽上的鹿角被认为具有某种神秘的力量，可以保护死者的灵魂。

has an impossibly long protruding tongue, which falls from the mouth like a necktie.

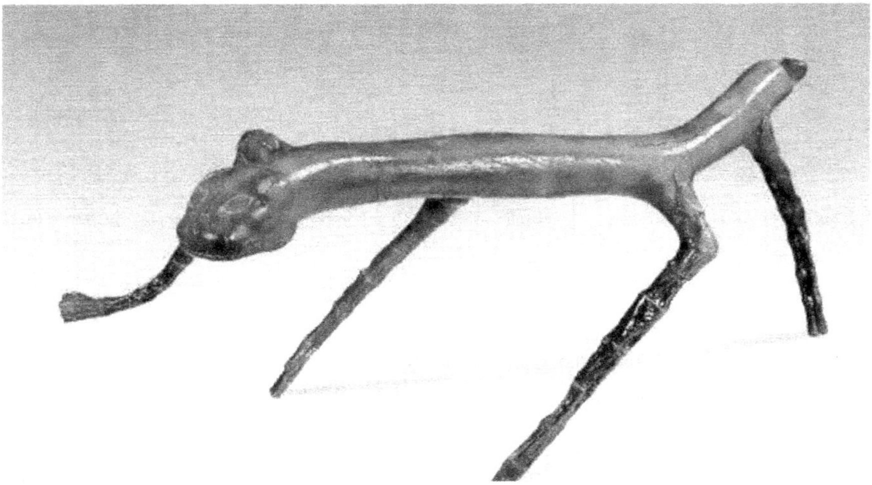

The Root Carving of an Auspicious Animal①
(Jingzhou Museum)

This root carving was unearthed at the Tomb No. 1 of Mashan, Jiangling in 1982. It is the earliest root carving art discovered in China. It has a tiger's head and four uneven limbs. This dragon-like creature is carved with a cicada at the top of the rear facing leg, a dragon biting a phoenix on the front facing leg, a long snake climbing up the withered front back leg, and a small snake biting a frog on the rear back leg. This strange shape and decoration show the religious and philosophical mystery of the Chu people. It is both a rare piece of artifact that acted as a guardian of the tomb.

The painting on the inner coffin of Marquis Yi of Zeng was filled with weird sense of witchcraft and was a visual expression of the southern myths and legends represented by the Chinese classic *Shan Hai Jing*.

---

① 根雕辟邪(荆州博物馆), 1982 年出土于江陵马山 1 号楚墓。根雕胎, 髹红漆, 是目前我国发现的最早的根雕艺术品。辟邪虎头曲身, 四肢长短不一, 四肢上浮雕蛇、蛇吃蜥蜴、蜥蜴吃鸟、蝉等, 这奇特的造型与装饰向人们展示出楚人的某种宗教、哲学之谜。它既是一件难得的艺术品, 又是墓葬的守护神器。

Deities on the Lacquered Inner Coffin of Marquis Yi Tomb in the late Warring States Period (Collected in Hubei Provincial Museum)

On the sides of the coffin are two rows of bird-man figures, armed with menacing weapons, presumably to ward off unwanted intruders to the marquis' sanctuary. They could be protective deities or shamans in professional gear. The complex maze of bird, snake, and human-headed configurations that fill the remaining panels of the coffin must signify various good and bad forces or deities relating to death and the afterlife.

Demons and Deities on the Lacquered Inner Coffin from Marquis Yi Tomb (Hubei Provincial Museum)

Figures resembling the deities on the Silk Manuscript from Zidanku appeared in the lacquered inner coffin of Marquis Yi of Zeng State. On the sides of the coffin are two rows of bird-man figures, armed with menacing weapons, presumably to ward off unwanted intruders to the marquis's sanctuary. They could be protective deities or shamans in professional gear. The complex maze of birds, snakes, and human-headed configurations that fill the remaining panels must signify various good and bad forces or deities relating to death and the afterlife.

Birds, snakes, and deer (often symbolized by their antlers), together with quasi-human or feline figures, are the main protagonists in some Chu deity representations.

Chu iconography includes a diversity of figures that can be interpreted as spirits or deities, from the figures on the inner coffin of Zeng Hou Yi to the dragon-imps on the coffin of the Lady Dai, from the multi-headed, multi-limbed peripheral figures of the Chu Silk Manuscript to the human-animal composites of the Mawangdui Silk Banner.

Chu customs and beliefs survive today in poetry (the *Chu Ci*, or *the Songs of the South*) as well as artifacts, revealing a mythology populated by an imaginative pantheon of demons and deities that inspired complex rituals with the requisite regalia.

The bird-snake, feline-snake, and shaman-snake combinations have often been considered as identifying features of Chu art, although their occurrence was not confined to Chu art alone. It is with this unwavering commitment to portraying real and mythical images in concrete or pictorial

The Lacquered Garment Box with the Design of Houyi Shooting down 9 Suns from Zeng Hou Yi Tomb
(Hubei Provincial Museum)

On the cover of the box there are two pairs of trees, birds, the Archer Hou Yi and radiating circles. The scene depicts the myth of the archer Hou Yi who saved the universe by shooting down the nine suns that appeared simultaneously in the sky. Along one edge of the cover of the lacquered suitcase there were intertwined serpents with human heads, a motif for the gods Fuxi and Nvwa, the progenitors in Chinese myth. On the edges of the cover there were trees, birds, animals, an archer and radiating circles, which depicted the myth of the archer Hou Yi who saved the universe by shooting down the nine suns that appeared simultaneously in the sky one day.

images, the abstract ideas of the universe or the fantastic tales and deities in ancient Chinese myth had been inspired by Chu art for the rapid development of both secular and religious sculpture and painting in China. This systematic portrayal of abstract beliefs and fantastic deities in art paved the way for the representations in Buddhist and Taoist art of the ensuing Han and Tang dynasties.

Chapter 3

Chu Beliefs in Jade Wares

According to the famous Chinese classic *Shuo Wen Jie Zi* (*Origin of Chinese Characters* by *Xu Shen*), "jade is the beautiful stone with five virtues."① The four most famous gem stones in China are Hetian jade in Xinjiang, Dushan jade in Henan, Xiuyan jade in Liao Ning, and Turquoise in Hubei②.

The most prominent early use was the crafting of the Six Ritual Jades③: bi, cong, huang, hu, gui, and zhang, which were presumed to symbolize political power or religious authority and thought to represent the sky, the earth, and the four directions respectively by the time of the composition of the *Rites of Zhou*. In the Xia, Shang, and Western Zhou dynasties, the rulers established a system of using ritual jades to consolidate their political power.

3.1 Belief in Jade Wares of Shijiahe Culture

The earliest few jade wares found in the middle reaches of the Yangtze

① 东汉许慎《说文解字》:"玉也，石之美者，有五德：润泽以温，仁之方也；鳃理自外，可以知中，义之方也；其声舒扬，专以远闻，智之方也；不桡而折，勇之方也；锐廉而不忮，絜之方也。"

② 中国四大宝石：和田玉、独山玉、岫岩玉、绿松石。

③ 六瑞。

River were in the Daxi Culture period. During the Shijiahe Culture period①, the jade industry developed rapidly and became a professional production.

Shijiahe Culture was named after the Shijiahe ruins in Tianmen Hubei dating from about 4, 800 to 4, 200 years ago. It is the largest Neolithic settlement site with a total area of more than 1. 2 million square meters and the most complete preservation in the middle reaches of the Yangtze River. The Shijiahe ruins are mainly distributed in Hubei, southwestern Henan and northern Hunan. The northernmost part can be extended to Zheng and Luo areas on the south bank of the Yellow River. The Shijiahe ruins are composed of dozens of sites such as Dengjiawan Ruin, Tucheng Ruin, Xiaojiawuji Ruin, etc.

As the highest representative of the social and cultural development in the middle reaches of the Yangtze River, the archaeological work in the core area of the Shijiahe ruins has achieved a series of major achievements, refreshing people's understanding of the civilized process in the middle reaches of the Yangtze River. The civilized process there had experienced the stages of Youziling Culture, Qujialing Culture and Shijiahe Culture. Its cultural influence spread to the upper and lower reaches of the Yangtze River and the middle and lower reaches of the Yellow River and played an important role in the process of Chinese civilization. The archaeological work was listed as one of the Ten Chinese Archaeological Discoveries in 2016.

① 石家河文化，石家河文化是中国长江中游地区的青铜文化，年代距今约4800—4200年。因湖北天门石家河遗址群而得名。主要分布在湖北、豫西南和湘北一带，最北处可扩展至黄河南岸的郑洛地区，为承袭屈家岭文化演变而来。该文化出现如石家河遗址群，由邓家湾、土城、肖家屋脊等数十处遗址组成。该文化已经发现有青铜块、玉器、祭祀遗迹以及类似于文字的刻划符号和城址，表明它已经进入文明时代。

During the Shijiahe Culture period, the Shijiahe ruins together with the contemporaneous Taosi ruins, Shijie ruins and Baodun ruins formed a cultural highland and a cultural circle, which interacted with each other and played a huge impact on the formation of Chinese civilization.

Nearly 300 pieces of jade wares were unearthed in Shijiahe. A total of 157 jade articles were found in the Xiaojiawuji of Tianmen, Hubei.

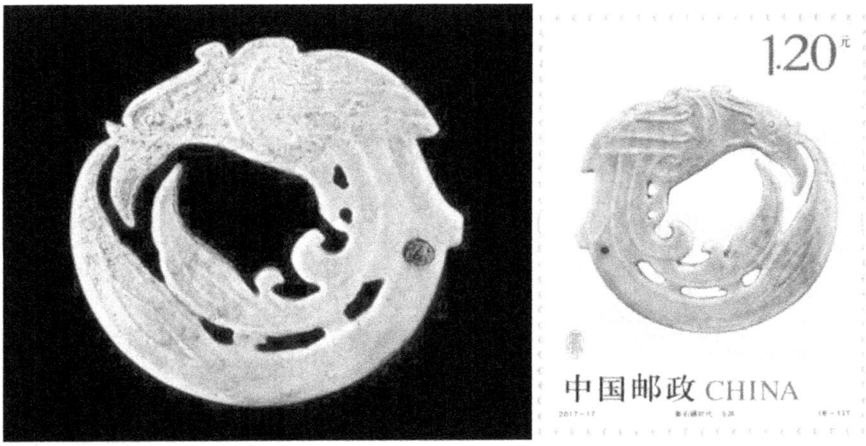

Jade Phoenix of Shijiahe Culture①
(National Museum of China)

This jade phoenix was unearthed in Luojia Bailing Site, Shijiahe Town of Tianmen City, Hubei Province in 1955. This jade phoenix is the jade ware of the late Neolithic Age in about 4, 800 to 4, 400 years ago. This jade phoenix was the earliest image of the phoenix in archaeological discovery. Its phoenix pattern has influenced the development of the phoenix art in China for thousands of years. This piece of jade phoenix adopts the method of thin ground relief and reflects the superb level of jade production.

① 石家河文化玉凤，现藏于中国国家博物馆。1955 年湖北省天门市石家河镇罗家柏岭遗址出土。这件玉凤距今约 4800—4400 年，是新石器时代晚期的玉佩。从目前考古材料得知，石家河文化出土的玉凤是目前所知较早的凤形象，开凤纹之先河，其造型影响了中国后来几千年凤鸟艺术的发展。这件玉凤采用减地阳刻法，体现了高超的玉器制作水平。

Jade Avatar①

The mysterious jade head was unearthed in Tanjialing, Tianmen, Hubei Provice. It has protruding eyes, tusks, eagle-hooked nose, which are inherited by the image of witches. The jade avatar is hollow. It may be used in religious activities.

① 玉人头像，谭家岭出土的神秘头像，其眼目凸出，獠牙、鹰钩鼻，这些都为后来神权人物和巫师的形象所继承。玉人头像内空，管径较大，可能为装柄之用，应用于祭祀等宗教活动中。

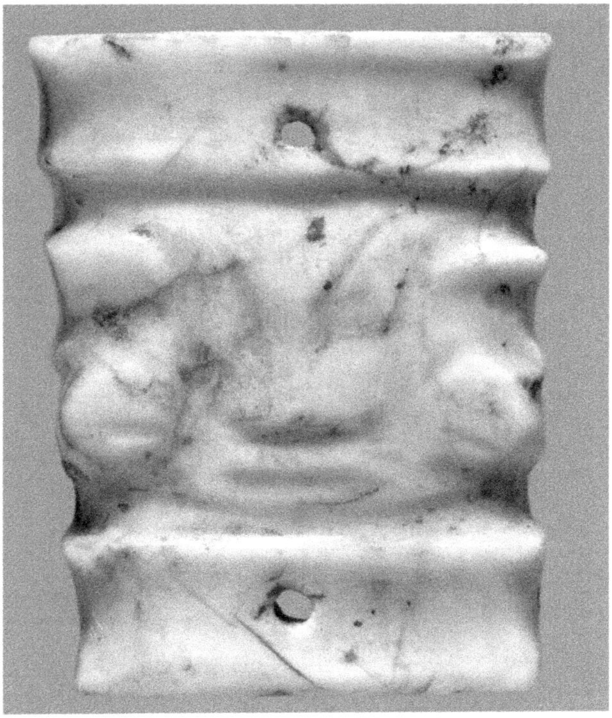

Jade Carving with Human Face①
(National Museum of China)

The jade carving with human face is the representative of Shijiahe Culture, which was unearthed in Luojia Bailing, Tianmen, Hubei Province in 1955. The face-shaped jade carving wears a flat crown, and under the crown is the face with a wide nose and large ears. There is a small hole in the center of the crown and neck. The function of the face-shaped jade ornaments is considered to be related to the primitive religion. Some scholars believe that these statues were used to communicate with the gods to get their blessing.

① 人面形玉雕，中国国家博物馆馆藏。人面形玉雕是石家河文化的代表，1955年湖北天门罗家柏岭出土。该人面形玉雕头戴平顶冠，冠下雕一人面，宽鼻方脸，大耳。头冠与颈部正中各有一小孔。对于石家河人面形玉饰的功能，被认为与原始宗教有关；有学者认为，这些人面雕像或许是巫师像，可以在通神时佩带，通过佩带这些人像，可以与神沟通，得到神灵庇佑。

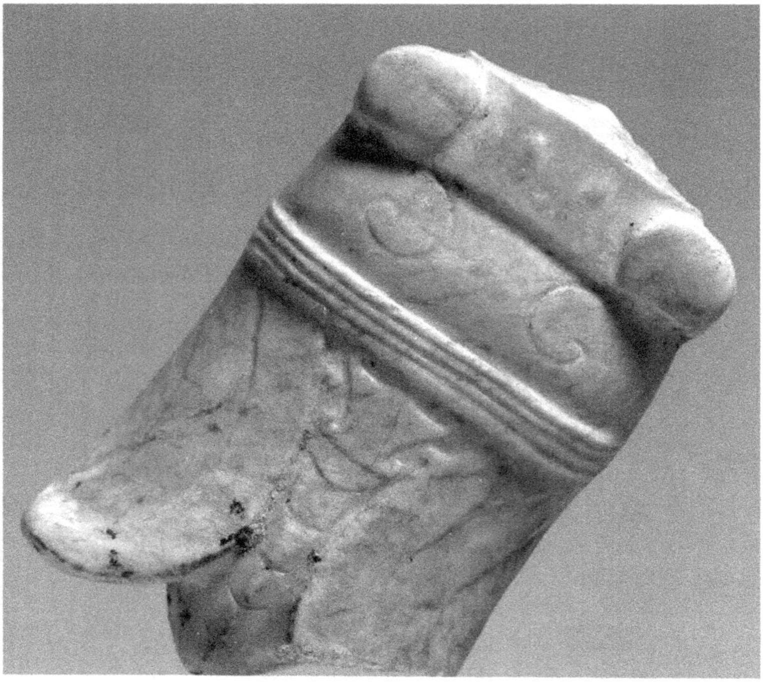

Cicada-shaped Jade Carving①
(National Museum of China)

The jade ware was unearthed at the site of the Xiaojiawuji of the late Shijiahe Culture of the Neolithic Age in Tianmen, Hubei Province.

Jade cicada was deeply loved by people in ancient times and was discovered not only in Shijiahe cultural ruins, but also found in Liangzhu Culture and Hongshan cultural relic sites. Because the cicadas can transform, the ancient people regarded it as a worm that could be regenerated. This jade cicada may be used to communicate with gods in religious activities.

Cicada is one of the most common animal images unearthed in the Shijiahe Culture. It has a fixed shape and is a relatively mature jade species.

---

① 蝉形佩，中国国家博物馆馆藏，新石器时代石家河文化晚期玉器，于湖北省天门肖家屋脊遗址出土。玉蝉在古代深受人们的喜爱，不但在石家河文化遗址中有大量的玉蝉，而且在良渚文化和红山文化遗址中也有发现。因为蝉能够蜕变，古人视蝉为能超脱和再生的神虫。此玉蝉的用途可能是佩带或缀于某物体上，在祭祀等宗教活动中作为一种通神的工具。蝉是石家河文化玉器中出土数量最多的一种动物形象。

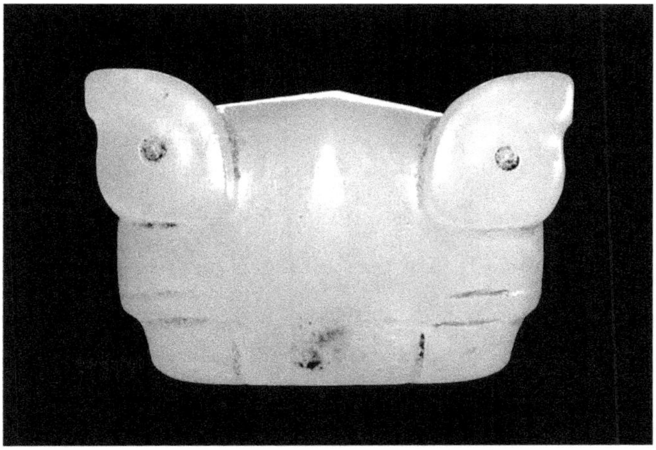

Jade Tiger Head①
(National Museum of China)

The jade tiger head is one of the representative forms of the Shijiahe Culture, which is only second to that of the jade cicadas. A total of 9 pieces were unearthed at the Xiaojiawuji site. In ancient China, the tiger was a symbol of bravery and invincibility as well as a mythical beast that connected man and gods.

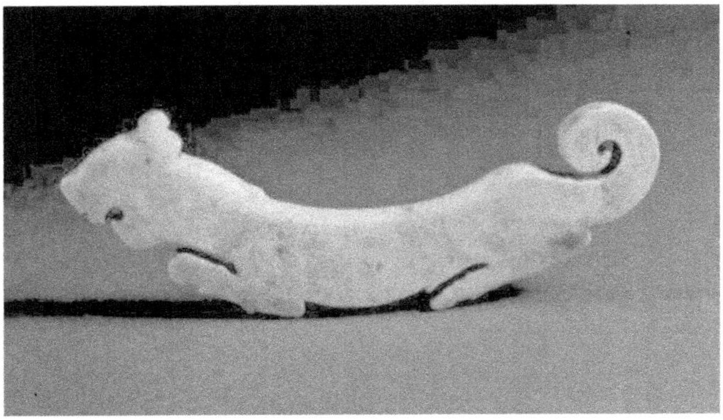

Jade Tiger of the Shijiahe Culture
(National Museum of China)

① 玉虎头，现藏于中国国家博物馆。虎头是石家河文化玉器的代表器形之一，数量仅次于蝉，在肖家屋脊遗址共出土了9件。在中国古代，虎是神威勇猛和不可战胜的象征，也是沟通人与神关系的神兽。

3.2　Jade Wares in Chu State

During the Spring and Autumn Period, the technology of producing jade products had made great progress in the middle reaches of the Yangtze River. The jade articles unearthed from the Chu tombs of Xichuan of the middle and late Spring and Autumn Period in Henan Province reflected the level of jade production at that time.

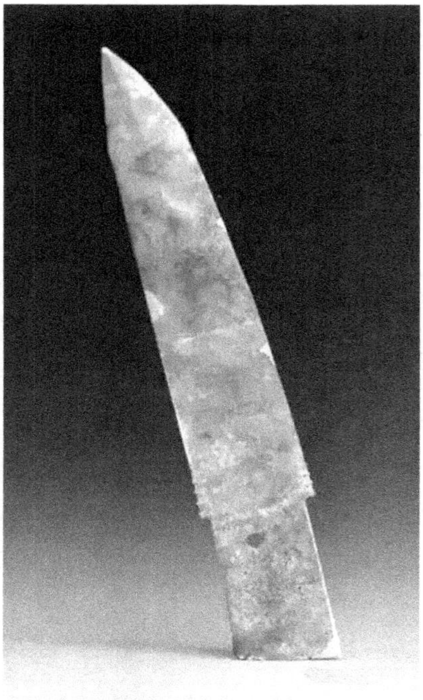

Jade Dagger Axe of the Shang Dynasty①
(Hubei Provincial Museum)

① 1974 年武汉市黄陂区盘龙城李家嘴三号墓出土的商代前期大玉戈，在商代玉器中十分罕见，堪称“玉戈之王”。大玉戈的出现，证明盘龙城在商代历史上占有重要地位。2002 年被列为中国首批禁止出国(境)展览文物。

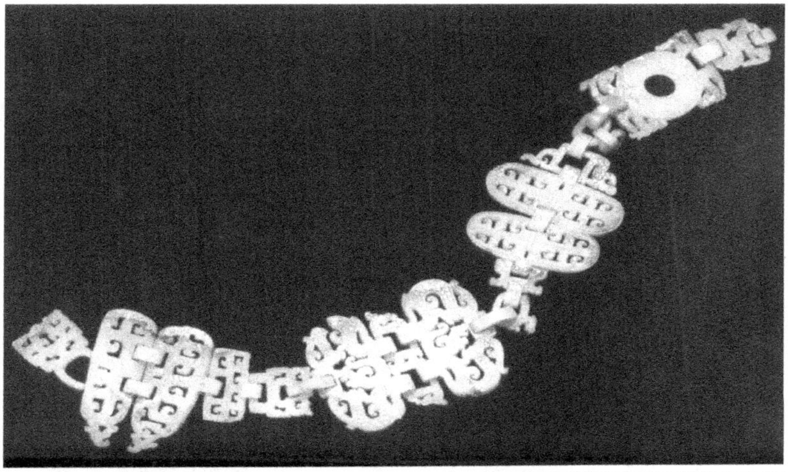

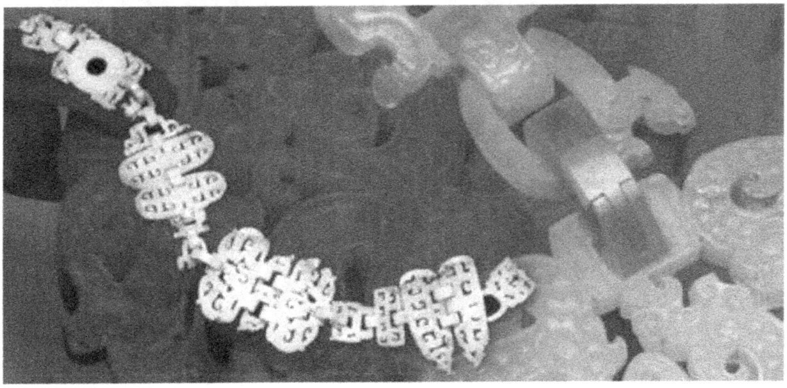

Jade Pendant of Marquis Yi of Zeng①
(Hubei Provincial Museum)

This jade ornament was unearthed in the tomb of Marquis Yi of Zeng State of the early Warring States Period in Suizhou, Hubei Province. This jade ornament or pendant with dragons and phoenixes was carved from five pieces of jade with 3 joins. The whole pendant is about 48 cm long in the shape of a dragon. There are thirty-seven dragons, seven phoenixes and ten snakes carved in this jade pendant. It is a collection of carving, openwork, flat carving, intaglio and other jade carving techniques.

① 曾侯乙十六节龙凤玉挂饰，现藏于湖北省博物馆，1978 年出土于湖北省随州市擂鼓墩战国早期墓葬曾侯乙墓。十六节龙凤玉佩由五块玉石采用分雕连接技术雕刻而成，由三个活环将十六节分别被雕琢成龙、凤、璧的玉佩连成可以拆卸的一组玉挂饰。全器呈龙形，长 48 厘米，十六节玉佩共雕琢有三十七条龙、七只凤及十条蛇，集分雕连接、透雕、平雕、阴刻等玉雕工艺于一身，为古代玉雕中罕见的精品。

It was the heyday of jade production in the middle reaches of the Yangtze River during the Warring States Period. Many fine jade articles were unearthed from the Chu tombs and the tomb of Marquis Yi of Zeng State. More than 300 pieces of jade articles were unearthed from the tomb of Marquis Yi,

Jade Mask①
(Jingzhou Museum)

This unique funeral jade mask was unearthed in August 1997 in the Chu Tomb of the Warring States Period in Qinjiashan, Jingzhou. The owner of the tomb is a female of the noble class of Chu State. This jade mask has an oval face and the hair and the mustache are centre parting, which is quite similar to the wood figurines unearthed in Jingzhou. It is an important material for studying Chu Culture.

① 玉覆面，藏于荆州博物馆。这件独特的丧葬用具玉覆面，1997 年 8 月出土于荆州秦家山二号战国中期楚墓。墓主人为女性，为楚国贵族。这件玉覆面的面部轮廓为瓜子脸，发、髭皆为中分式，与荆州出土的木俑颇为相近，是研究楚文化的重要实物资料。

among which four sections of dragon and phoenix jade, and sixteen sections of dragon and phoenix jade are called the crown of the Warring States jade.

Judging from the jade articles unearthed from the Chu tombs of Yutaishan and Wangshan in Jiangling, Zhaojiahu in Dangyang, No. 2 Tomb of Baoshan in Jingmen, etc., the Chu people wore jade ornaments according to the aristocratic classes based on the custom in the Central Plains during the Warring States Period. The jade artifacts unearthed from the Chu tombs of the Warring States exemplified the interest in exquisite and intricate decoration and interlace with novelty and diversity.

3. 3 Famous Stories About Jade in Chu State

3. 3. 1 Six Kinds of Treasures

The historical classic *Guo Yu* recorded the story of how Chu people valued the Jade Hang.

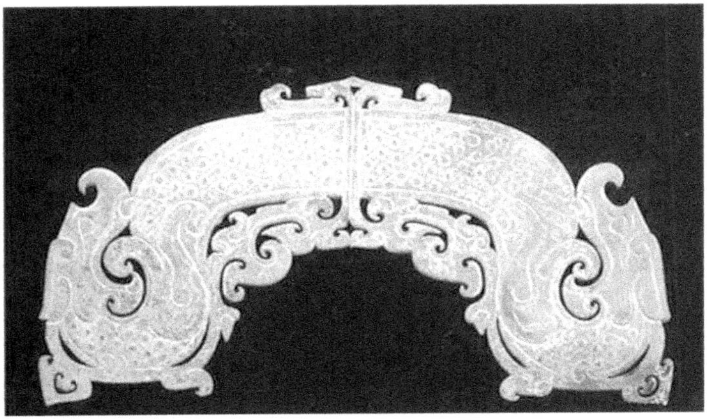

Jade Hang from Chu Tomb in Changfeng Anhui
(Anhui Provincial Museum)

During King Zhao's reign, Wang Sunyu visited Jin State. During the banquet, Zhao Jianzi, a prime minister who wore the jade pendent to show the wealth of Jin State, asked Wang Sunyu how long the Jade Hang had been kept as the treasure in Chu. Wang Sunyu responded that "The Chu people had never valued Jade as a treasure but valued three kinds of treasures, namely, the minister Guanshefu, the historian Yi Xiang, and the Yunmeng lake. The white jade is only the plaything, how can it be the treasure? There are six kinds of treasures in a country. The first one should be wise kings and virtue officials. The second should be the jade which is used to offer sacrifice to the gods to ask for harvest. The third should be the tortoise which is used to ask for fortune. The fourth is the pearls used to ward off fire disaster. The fifth should be the copper which is used to make weapons to defense the enemy. And the last should be mountains and rivers. Is the jade that makes only noise valuable? Though the Chu people live in brutal places, we never take jade as the only treasure."①

This old story gives us the enlightenment of what is most valuable for a country.

---

① 《国语·楚语》原文：王孙圉聘于晋，定公飨之。赵简子鸣玉以相，问于王孙圉曰："楚之白珩犹在乎？"对曰："然。"简子曰："其为宝也，几何矣？"曰："未尝为宝。楚之所宝者，曰观射父，能作训辞，以行事于诸侯，使无以寡君为口实。又有左史倚相，能道训典，以叙百物，以朝夕献善败于寡君，使寡君无忘先王之业；又能上下说乎鬼神，顺道其欲恶，使神无有怨痛于楚国。又有薮曰云，连徒洲，金、木、竹、箭之所生也。龟、珠、角、齿，皮、革、羽、毛，所以备赋，以戒不虞者也；所以共币帛，以宾享于诸侯者也。若诸侯之好币具，而导之以训辞，有不虞之备，而皇神相之。寡君其可以免罪于诸侯，而国民保焉。此楚国之宝也。若夫白珩，先王之玩也，何宝之焉？"圉闻国之宝，六而已：圣能制议百物，以辅相国家，则宝之；玉足以庇荫嘉谷，使无水旱之灾，则宝之；龟足以宪臧否，则宝之；珠足以御火灾，则宝之；金足以御兵乱，则宝之；山林薮泽足以备财用，则宝之。若夫哗嚣之美，楚虽蛮夷，不能宝也。"

3.3.2 The Story of Jade Heshi Bi

Jade Bi Unearthed from Chu Tomb in Xiongjiazhong, Jingzhou Hubei①

In *Han Fei Zi* there is another story of jade in Chu State. In the Spring and Autumn Period, there was a jade craftsman named Bianhe in Chu State. He once got a piece of unpolished gem in Mountain Jingshan and presented it to King Li and later to King Wu of Chu. They thought he was cheating and chopped off his left and right foot with the crime of bullying. Bianhe was so depressed that he cried his eyes to bleeding until King Wen came to him. King Wen ordered the craftsman to cut off this piece of unpolished gem and got a wonderful jade. Later the Jade Bi made with this gem stone was given

① 2006年8月以来，考古人员对荆州熊家冢楚墓排葬坑及车马坑进行发掘，发掘了迄今发现的中国同时期最长的特大型车马坑，以及呈“一”字形排列的30多座小型车马坑，殉葬墓92座。现有发掘成果表明，熊家冢是中国已发掘楚墓中规格最高、规模最大、布局最完整的一处楚国高等级贵族墓葬。

the name Heshi Bi.

The story of Heshi Bi took place in Chu State, which shows that the State of Chu abounded in jade and the Chu people were masters of jade production.

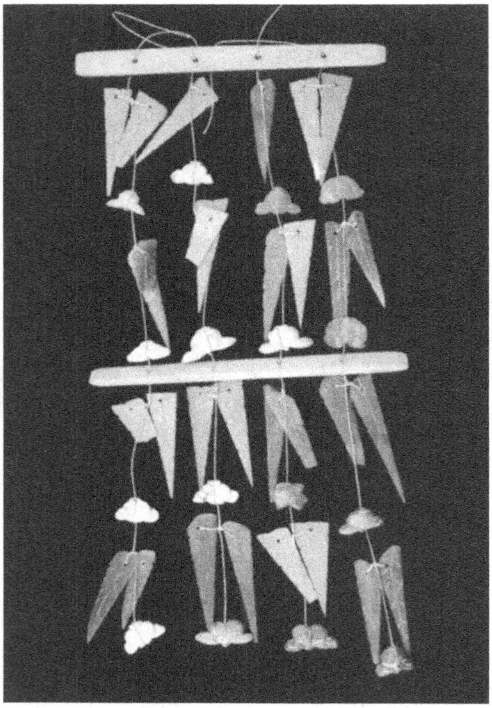

Jade Pendant①(a Set of Jade Pendant Used to Decorate the Dressing and Forbid Quick Steps) of the Ming Dynasty
(Hubei Provincial Museum)

---

① 玉禁步渊源于先秦时代的组玉佩，身份高贵者行步舒缓以见其尊，故有节步之意。这组于2001年出土于湖北省梁庄王墓的玉禁步，由49件玉饰(32片玉叶、16件串饰及1件玉珩)组成。它不但精致华贵，而且将众多有吉祥寓意的饰物归为一体，其中包括：32片玉叶，代表金枝玉叶；4只玉桃，寓意福寿平安；4件玉瓜，象征瓜熟蒂落；2条玉鱼，象征富贵有余；4个玛瑙制成的石榴，象征多子多福；2只玛瑙鸳鸯，寓意百年和美。整件组佩精美绝伦。

Chapter 4

Chu Power in Bronze Vessels

The quest of power for Chu Kings was a popular subject for ancient storytellers and historians. In the quest of power, bronze plays an important role. In *Zuo Zhuan*, two arrogant but successful Chu rulers, King Zhuang and King Ling, suggested the time had come for Zhou King to pass the sacred bronze "Nine Caldrons" on to Chu.

Bronze vessels are some of the most important pieces of ancient Chinese art. The majority of surviving Chinese ancient bronze artifacts is for ritual rather than practical use. Even weapons like daggers and axes had a sacrificial meaning, symbolizing the heavenly power of the ruler.

4.1 Chu Power in Bronze Vessels

The success of King Xiongqu of Chu State attacking the State of E made the copper mine the source of the development of Chu. In the reign of King Cheng, the State of Chu moved northward to get involved into the mainstream civilization in the north and eastward to get control of mines along the middle reaches of the Yangtze River. At that time, the copper mines in Chu State exceeded that in any other country in quantity and scale.

Tonglvshan Ancient Copper Mine Relic Sites①

The ancient mining and refining furnaces show that the copper smelting process in the Spring and Autumn Period reached the highest level in the world at that time. This ancient mining and smelting site here is the highest level and best preserved among similar sites all over the world. It is a precious cultural heritage of mankind.

① 大冶铜绿山古铜矿遗址发现于 1973 年，是迄今为止我国保存最好、最完整，采掘时间最早、冶炼水平最高、规模最大、保存最完整的一处古铜矿遗址。铜绿山古铜矿遗址于 1982 年被列为全国重点文物保护单位，1987 年由国务院申报有关联合国教科文组织列为国际遗产。

The Chu people adopted the smelting technology in Yang & Yue states and the casting technology in Sui State and improved them in production, which made Chu take lead in bronze production in the north.

In the Chu Tomb of the Autumn and Spring Period in Shanwan Xiangyang, there were Ding of King Cheng of Deng State① and Fu of Shangruo② unearthed. In the Tomb of Xiasi Xichuan, there were Ba-style Sword③, Halberd Used by Lord Liao④, Fu Owned by Marquis Cai⑤ and Bell Owned by King Lv⑥ excavated. These bronze wares were treasured by the Chu people, which reflected the openness of Chu Culture.

In the King Wu and King Wen periods, the Chu people followed the bronze production in the north but made innovation according to their own practical requirement, subjective position and aesthetic taste.

The Sheng Ding⑦ was round with narrowed waist, flat bottom, outward-flung ears, and 4 or 6 attached animals. This unique style is different from the kind in the north.

For the Yu Ding⑧, it was first imitated from the kind in the north and later it was added the buckle and handle on the lid.

In the ritual system of the Zhou Dynasty, Ding and Gui should be used in pairs in ceremony. The Chu people abided by this rule at the beginning and later changed it by matching Ding and Fu in the early and middle Autumn and Spring Period.

① 邓公乘鼎
② 上都府簠
③ 巴式剑
④ 鄝子之用戟
⑤ 蔡侯簠
⑥ 吕王钟
⑦ 升鼎
⑧ 于鼎

Nine Ding and Eight Gui Vessels of Marquis Yi of Zeng (Hubei Provincial Museum)

According to the ritual books, the King of Zhou used 9 ding and 8 gui vessels, a marquis was allowed to use 7 dings and 6 guis, a baron could use 5 dings and 3 guis, a nobleman was allowed to use 3 dings and 2 guis.

In fact, Fu was not a necessity for the Chu people, but the Chu nobilities replaced Gui with Fu to make their ritual system different from that in the Zhou Dynasty. In shape, Ding and Gui are all round, while Fu is square. The Chu people changed the match of Ding and Gui into Ding and Fu, which reflected their unique aesthetic taste and character of pursuing novelty.

In 1978, a set of 7 pieces of ding, which were cast by the lost-wax technique, were unearthed from the Chu Tomb of Xiasi, Xichuan of Henan Province. Engraved with the characters "Wangzi Wu" (Prince Wu), this set of bronze vessels belong to Chu State in the Spring and Autumn Period. Prince Wu Ding① became the standard instrument for studying Chu Culture.

The overall shape of the Prince Wu Ding changed the style of magnificence and savage beauty of the Shang and Zhou bronze vessels, and applied the Chu people's preference of gentleness and delicacy like woman's slim waist to the

① 1978 年，河南省淅川县下寺楚墓中出土了一套 7 件用失蜡法铸造的青铜列鼎，鼎上铭刻有“王子午”字样，是春秋时期楚国的青铜器。王子午鼎成为研究楚文化的标准器物。王子午鼎整体曲线造型一改商周青铜鼎硬朗的风格，把楚人爱细腰的偏好应用到青铜礼器的铸造上，使厚重的青铜鼎尽显柔美。其铸造使用了当时先进的焊接技术和失蜡铸造技术。先以失蜡法铸出 6 条立体龙形怪兽，然后将其焊接于鼎身，显示了很高的铸造水准。优美的造型、精细的纹饰、浪漫奇诡的题材，正是楚国文化艺术的突出特征。

bronze casting. Six decorative dragon-shaped monsters were cast into three-dimensional mold with advanced lost-wax casting technique, and then were welded to the body of the Ding. Beautiful shapes, fine patterns, and exotic themes are the prominent features of the Chu culture and art.

Ding of Prince Wu①
(Henan Museum)

Prince Wu was the son of King Zhuang of Chu State. The inscription in the vessel consists of 83 characters which write "Prince Wu casts this food vessel for offering sacrifices to our ancestor King Wen and for swearing ceremonies of forming alliance. Because of my benevolent rule, I am loved and respected by all the people of Chu State. It is hoped that the later generations will regard this as the standard of their conduct and behavior."

---

① 楚庄王之子、楚国令尹"王子午"墓中所出7件列鼎之一。鼎身为束腰平底状，侈耳、蹄足，口沿攀附6条龙形怪兽，器腹满饰半浮雕的夔纹和窃曲纹。内腹与盖有铭文85字，大意为"王子午自铸铜鼎，以祭先祖文王，进行盟祀，我施德政于民，因而受到尊重，望子孙后代以此为准则"。周代一些用于祭祀和宴饮的器物，被赋予特殊意义，这就是所谓"藏礼于器"。鼎原来是炊器，后来成为礼器中最重要的器种之一，簋是盛器，与铜鼎组合用于礼仪祭祀中。周朝的奴隶主贵族用鼎有严格规定，分为一鼎、三鼎、五鼎、七鼎、九鼎五个等级，其中，一鼎、三鼎是"士"级贵族在不同场合使用；五鼎是"卿大夫"级贵族使用；七鼎是"诸侯"级别的贵族使用；九鼎则是君王专用。这些鼎往往形制相似而大小不同，尺寸依次递减，通常称为"列鼎"。而簋则是与鼎相配合的，四簋与五鼎相配；六簋与七鼎相配；八簋与九鼎相配。

Wangzi Wu Ding from Xiasi of the Xichuan Burial Ground
(National Museum of China)
(The seven intricately decorated high-legged cauldrons of Wu placed in Weizi Ping's tomb all had the word "Ping" scratched into their surfaces. Whether Weizi Ping received Wu's bronzes as an emblem of merit during his lifetime or as a lineage debt paid at his death remains a mystery.)

Great Ding Engraved with "Zhu Ke"①
(Anhui Museum)

This Ding was unearthed from the Tomb of the Chu King of Warring States Period (475 BC-221 BC) at Zhujiaji, Shou County (Now in Huainan City) in 1933. This huge Ding represents the perfect combination of strength and momentum, which shows the ambition of its masters. This tripod is the most majestic among thousands of pieces of Chu bronze Ding, so it is also known as the Great Bronze Ding. On the mouth of this Ding, there are inscribed with 12 characters of "Zhu Ke made...". On the forefoot and abdomen there are engraved with two words "An Bang", an auspicious wish for the state at that time. It is the only confirmed tomb of the King You of Chu.

① 铸客大铜鼎，安徽博物院馆藏，战国时期楚国青铜器，1933 年寿县朱家集李三孤堆楚王墓出土。中国首批禁止出国(境)展览文物。铸客大铜鼎体量巨大，造型设计上处处追求力量与气势的完美结合，无不呈现出其主人拔山盖世的雄心壮志。此鼎在数千件楚器中最为雄伟，所以又被称为大铜鼎。鼎口处阴刻铭文"铸客为……"等十二字，鼎的前足和腹下均刻有"安邦"二字。李三孤堆墓群为楚幽王墓，是迄今发现的唯一可以确认的楚国国王墓。

Zhu Ke Ding①
(Anhui Provincial Museum)
Bronze wares of the Warring States Period, unearthed in the tomb of Chu King in Zhujiaji of Shou County, Anhui Province in 1933

4.2　The Story of the Quest for Power②

In Chinese culture, the possession of "ding" is often associated with power and dominion over the land. Therefore, ding is often used as an implicit symbolism for power and authority. The Early Western Zhou Dynasty underwent a political and cultural change. King Wu of Zhou believed that the addiction to wine led the king in the Shang Dynasty to lose the Mandate of Heaven, thus caused the downfall of the Shang Dynasty. Therefore, food vessels ("ding" in particular) replaced wine vessels in importance③.

In Chinese idioms, "Wèn dǐng qīng zhòng" (inquiring the weight of

① 铸客升鼎，安徽省博物院藏，战国时期青铜器，1933 年安徽省寿县朱家集楚王墓出土。

② 问鼎轻重。

③ https://en.wikipedia.org/wiki/Chinese_ritual_bronzes

Ding) is a famous saying, which suggests Chu kings quest for power or "attempt to seize the throne".

Ding of King Xionghan of Chu State①
(Tianjin Museum)

This Ding was in unearthed from the Li San Gu Dui Tomb of King You of Chu in Zhujiaji (now Huainan City) in 1933. Sixty inscriptions in this Ding recorded the facts of King You of Chu used the seized weapons to cast this tripod to celebrate the victory and offer sacrifice.

In 613BC, during the reign of King Zhuang of Chu, the State of Chu became powerful once again. In 606BC, King Zhuang of Chu led his army to River Luoshui and demonstrated the morale of his army in the capital Luoyang of the Zhou Dynasty. The King of the Zhou Dynasty sent King Sunman to visit King Zhuang. King Zhuang inquired the size and the weight of the Ding,

① 楚王酓悍鼎，1933年寿县朱家集(今属淮南市)李三孤堆楚王墓出土，该鼎收藏于天津博物馆。该鼎上共有六十字铭文，记载了楚幽王为庆贺胜利用缴获的兵器铸成此鼎的经过并用于祭祀的史实。

intending to replace the reign of Zhou. King Sunman knew King Zhuang came for Zhou to pass the sacred "Jiu Ding"①(Nine Caldrons) on to Chu and said that Jiu Ding were too big and too old to estimate the weight. King Zhuang replied that "only the hooks of the Chu soldiers were enough to cast Jiu Ding". King Sunman said that "the rule of the world is not decided by the weight of Ding but by accumulation of power or virtue". King Zhuang of Chu was silenced by his remarks and withdrew from the territory of the Zhou Dynasty. But King Zhuang never stopped expanding the power and territory and later made himself one of the Five Hegemonies of the Spring and Autumn Period.

Bronze Jin (Altar Table) with Cloud Design
(Henan Provincial Museum)

Jin is a table for carrying wine vessels. This bronze Jin is the earliest one of all the bronze objects cast with the lost-wax casting technique unearthed from Xiasi of the Xichuan Burial Ground in China. Its body has several layers of cloud-shaped relief decorations supported by bronze stalks of various sizes, with twelve dragon-shaped animals climbing around and another twelve staying at the bottom as legs of the Jin. Because King Wu of the Zhou Dynasty believed that the addiction to wine led the King in Shang Dynasty to lose the Mandate of Heaven and caused the downfall of the Shang Dynasty, the table of carrying the

① The nine caldrons represented the Heavenly Mandate (Tian Ming), the right to rule the empire.

wine vessels was named as Jin to give a warning for wine addiction.

This bronze Jin with cloud pattern was excavated from Prince Wu's tomb, which was the earliest one of all the bronze objects cast with the lost-wax casting technique unearthed in China. The exquisite and complex craftsmanship showed the great wealth and power of the State of Chu at that period. The excavation of this bronze Jin dated back the history of China's lost-wax casting in 1100.

The Bronze Zun-Pan of Marquis Yi of Zeng
(Hubei Provincial Museum)

The intertwined serpentine configurations and the addition of animals on the walls or bases of vessels could be traced back to the Western Zhou Period, turning them into the complex openwork and intertwined ornaments on the bronzes seems to be a Chu trait. The production of this intricate openwork of serpentine creature probably inspired the development of a new casting technique—the lost-wax method to supplement the traditional section-mold casting technique used since ca. 1500 BCE.

4.3 Culture in Bronze Sword

According to archaeological findings, the number of burial swords in the Chu tombs of different classes is unmatched by other countries. This should be the reflection of the spirit of the Chu people in the tombs.

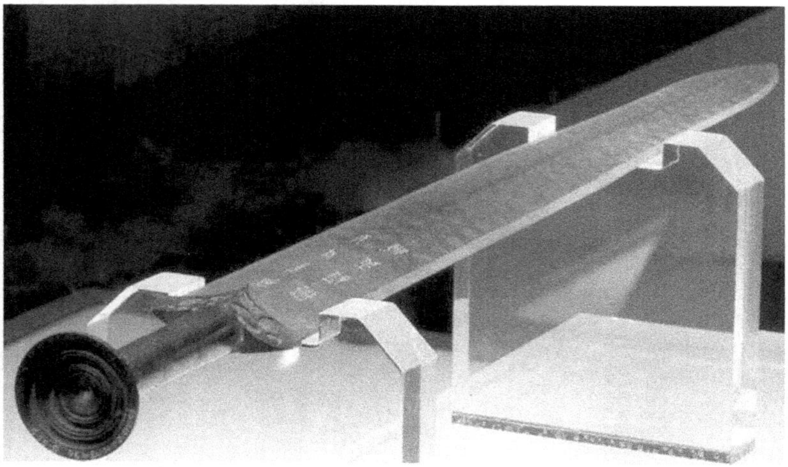

The Bronze Sword of King Goujian of Yue①
(Hubei Provincial Museum)

A state frequently engaged in wars, Yue developed wonderful weapons much admired by the central China. Some of these were probably not intended for practical use but instead were destined for ceremonial display or to be given as gift. This Sword of King Goujian of

① 举世闻名的越王勾践剑，春秋晚期越国青铜器，1965年12月出土于湖北省荆州市江陵县望山楚墓中，此剑长55.7厘米，宽4.6厘米，柄长8.4厘米，重875克，近剑格处有两行鸟篆铭文——“越王鸠浅(勾践)自乍(作)用剑”八字，证明此剑就是传说中的越王勾践剑。此剑历经两千四百余年，仍然纹饰清晰精美，锋利无比，加之“物以人名”，历史文化价值很高，被誉为“天下第一剑”。

Yue was excavated from the Chu tombs of Wangshan Jiangling in 1965, which might be a gift or trophy from Yue State.

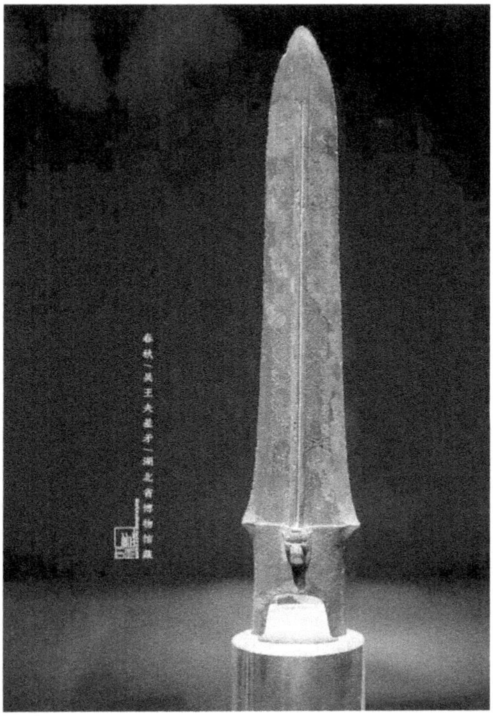

The Bronze Spear Inlaid with "Fuchai, King of Wu State" ①
(Hubei Provincial Museum)

The Bronze Spear of King Fuchai of Wu State was unearthed in No. 5 Chu Tomb of Mashan Jiangling in 1983. This spear is inlaid with gold inscription of "King Fuchai of Wu which had this spear made for his own use". It is a bronze treasure of the Spring and Autumn Period. How this spear comes to Chu is still open to further study.

The idiom of "Ke Zhou Qiu Jian" (Marking on the Boat to Retrieve the Sword) can tell the importance of sword for the Chu people:

---

① 吴王夫差矛于 1983 年在湖北省江陵县马山 5 号楚墓出土，是春秋末期吴国使用的兵器，是春秋时期一件青铜珍品。上面刻有"吴王夫差，自乍(作)用口(矛)"的错金铭文。中国多处出土夫差矛，夫差矛并非吴王夫差专用武器，而是夫差时期所铸青铜矛。越王勾践剑与吴王夫差矛是我国古代兵器中的"双璧"。至于吴王夫差矛怎样来到楚地的，尚待学术界进一步研究。

One day a man of the State of Chu was crossing a river by boat. His sword fell into the river accidently. He quickly cut a sign on the side of the boat and said "It is the place where my sword fell. I will get my sword back from here as soon as the boat stops." When the boat pulled into shore, he jumped into the river from the place where he marked to search his sword.

In this story, the boat has moved in the river while the lost sword has not. How foolish to search the lost sword like this!

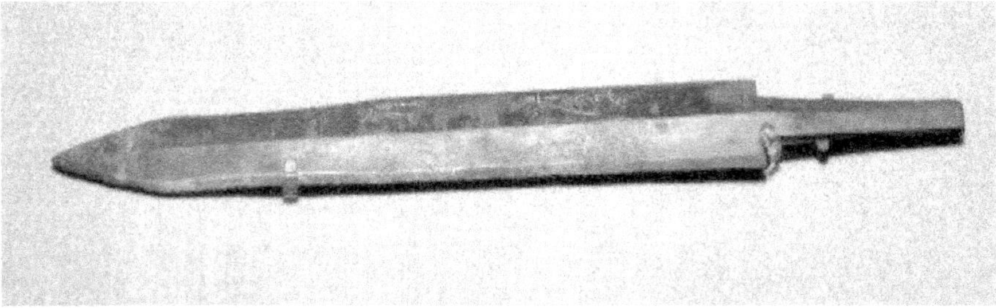

The Bronze Sword Inscribed with "Fan Yang Zhi Jin"① and Sheathed in an Ivory Scabbard Inlaid with Pearls
(Henan Provincial Museum)

Another story of "Gan Jiang Mo Ye" (The Story of Sword Gan Jiang and Sword Mo Ye) reflected the relationship of sword and Chu State. In a famous ancient Chinese mysterious novel "Sou Shen Ji" (The Stories of Ghosts and Monsters), there is a story of "Gan Jiang Mo Ye". Gan Jiang, a craftsman in the State of Wu in the Spring and Autumn Period, once cast swords for the King of Wu. One day he was asked to cast swords for the King of Chu. He casted two precious swords, one was named after his name "Gan Jiang", the

① 战国"繁阳之金"铜剑，1964 年洛阳房管局出土。剑鞘由象牙制成，剑保存完好，至今仍十分锋利。剑身有错铜蚊脚书 4 字"繁阳之金"。繁阳，战国时属楚地，在汝南鲖阳县(今新蔡县北)，这件铜剑的发现，证明繁阳是中国古代著名的产铜之地。

other was named after his wife's name "Mo Ye". He presented the sword "Mo Ye" to the King of Chu, and asked his wife to pass the sword "Gan Jiang" to his son. The King of Chu was angry with him and killed him. His son Meijianchi grew up and killed the King of Chu with the sword of "Gan Jiang" to take revenge.

The Bronze Warrior with a Sword on the Waist
(Hubei Provincial Museum)

Chapter 5

Chu Clothing in Silk Fabrics

Silk, as a symbol of ancient Chinese culture, has not only woven an excellent picture in the history of Chinese civilization but also made great contribution to the advancement of human being.

During the Spring and Autumn Period and the Warring States Period, the silk producing and embroidery industry of Chu State rose up and went ahead of other vassal states. The thinker Guan Zhong in the Spring and Autumn Period wrote in his *Guanzi—Xiao Kuang*① that Chu State "tribute silk to the Zhou court", indicating that the super quality of the silk produced by Chu.

Most of the silk fabrics and embroidery products of the Spring and Autumn Period and the Warring States Period were unearthed in the Chu tombs in Hubei and Hunan provinces.

In 1982, a large number of silk fabrics were unearthed from No. 1 Chu Tomb of Mashan in Jiangling, Hubei Province. The quality of the silk fabric fully demonstrates the superb skill and aesthetic taste of Chu's costume culture. This tomb is therefore known as the underground "silk treasure house" of the Pre-Qin Dynasty.

---

① 春秋时期的思想家管仲在《管子·小匡》中记道：楚国"贡丝于周室"。

5.1 Silk Weaving Technology

As long ago as the Neolithic Age, the Chinese ancestors had invented flat-weaving and figured-weaving techniques. The looming device represented the level of textile technology. In 1978, the excavation of the tomb of Marquis Yi of Zeng confirmed the existence of the looming device since there were some thick robes tied to the coffin.

A few silk sashes were unearthed from No. 1 Chu Tomb of Mashan in Jiangling, which should be woven with a waist looming machine①.

Brocade best reflected the highest level of Chu silk weaving technology. It is speculated that the colored brocade sash with paired beast unearthed from No. 1 Tomb of Wangshan, Jiangling should be woven with multi-heddle and multi-treadle looms.

According to the different requirements of softness, color and gloss, the silk fabric is generally processed by refining, dyeing and polishing②.

Refining③ is the preparation process before dyeing, which removes the impurities adhering to the fabric and makes it softer, purer and easier to color.

Dyeing process originated as a way of pursuing beauty in the primitive society and became a symbol of classes in the Spring and Autumn Period and the Warring States Period. The mineral dyes used in the Warring States Period were mainly produced in Jingzhou of Hubei Province, Chenxi of Hunan

① 多综多蹑织机。

② 根据对丝织物柔软度、色彩、光泽度等的不同要求，织物一般要经过练、染、研光等技术处理。

③ 练是丝织物在染色前的准备工作，练后的织物除去了表面附着的杂质，变得更加柔软、纯净，易于着色。

Province, and eastern Chongqing.

The Seal Engraved with "Zhong Zhi Shi Yin" (Seal of Court Textile Office)①
(Hunan Provincial Museum)

5.2 Silk & Embroidery Fabrics Unearthed in Chu State

Most of the silk fabrics and embroidery products found in the archaeological excavations are from the territory of the State of Chu. These objects showed that the silk weaving and embroidery technology in Chu State was ranked first among all the states in the Warring States Period, representing the highest level at that time.

Most of the silk fabrics and embroidery products of Chu State were

① 中织室印，20世纪40年代湖南长沙征集，现收藏于湖南省博物馆。"织室"是专管纺织的机构。这方古玺可说明在战国时期的楚国就已设有专门管理宫中纺织的机构和官员。仰天湖楚简中随葬众多纺织品的记载和湖北江陵马山楚墓中出土的大量精美纺织品，都说明楚国纺织业的发达。"中织室印"四字，布局匀称，形体秀健，笔画圆润，字形结构与长沙仰天湖出土的楚简文字相同，具有鲜明的战国楚系文字特征。

unearthed in the Chu tombs in Jiangling District of Hubei Province. Among them, the silk fabrics unearthed from Tomb No. 1 of Mashan in Jiangling can be divided into chiffon (yarn-dye silk fabric 绢), brocade (锦), leno (罗), damask (绮), yarn (gauze 纱), bengaline (绨), and bengaline (绦) according to different weaving techniques and organizational structures.①

Leno Embroidered with Dragons, Phoenixes and Tigers②
(Jingzhou Museum)

This silk fabric was unearthed from No. 1 Chu Tomb, Mashan of Jiangling in Hubei Province in 1982.

The tiger was embroidered with silk thread dyed with vermilion and dark gray. The vermilion is bright and dazzling, and the dark gray luster is pleasant. Over two thousand years, it still maintains excellent color fastness and color brilliancy.

---

① 楚国的丝织品和刺绣品实物大多出土于湖北江陵地区的楚墓。其中江陵马山一号墓出土的丝织品，按织造方法和组织结构不同，可以分为绢、锦、罗、绮、纱、绨、绦等。

② 龙凤虎纹绣罗，荆州博物馆馆藏。1982 年湖北省江陵马山 1 号楚墓出土。图案中的虎是用朱红和深灰两色的丝线绣成的，朱红色鲜艳夺目，深灰色光泽可人，虽历经两千多年，仍然保持极好的染色牢度和色彩。

The colors that can be seen in silk fabric of Chu State include indigo, yellow, red, purple, etc. Most of them were dyed with plant dyes. For example, indigo was extracted from the blue grass. In Chinese idiom "indigo comes out of blue but it is much darker than blue", blue refers to this kind of blue grass①. The color of indigo is bright and elegant, and it can withstand the sun and wash. In the bengaline (unearthed from the No. 1 Chu Tomb of Mashan in Jiangling) with the picture of driving and hunting, the hunter and driver was dyed in indigo, which is still shining after thousands of years.

The emergence of brocade is an important milestone in the history of Chinese silk, because it combines the excellent quality of silk with art, making silk not only a noble cloth but also a work of art and enhancing its historical value.

The eight types of silk fabrics unearthed from No. 1 Chu Tomb at Mashan in Jiangling were almost all kinds of silk fabrics of the Pre-Qin Dynasty. It is worth noting that the tomb owner of No. 1 Chu Tomb at Mashan was a woman of the class of Shi (a social stratum between senior officials and the common people in ancient China), therefore the silk fabric unearthed there did not necessarily represent the highest level of silk producing and embroidery in Chu State.

The patterns on the embroidered silk fabrics of Chu State can be roughly divided into four types: geometric patterns, plant patterns, animal patterns and character patterns.

---

① 楚国丝织品的用色可以见到靛蓝、黄、红、紫等，它们大多是用植物染成。靛蓝就是从蓝草中提取的，“青出于蓝而胜于蓝”，指的就是这种蓝草。靛蓝色牢度很好，能耐日晒和水洗，颜色鲜艳，古朴雅致。湖北江陵马山一号楚墓出土的田猎纹绦中，驾车狩猎人物的衣着就是靛蓝色，至今仍光彩照人。

Tao with Patterns of Diamond and Hexagon of the Warring States Period)①
(Jingzhou Museum, Unearthed from No. 1 Chu Tomb of Mashan, Jiangling)

Among the geometric patterns, the Chu people preferred the diamond pattern. They combined the wings and tails of the phoenix and the flowers to form a unique diamond pattern.

Another feature of the Chu-style embroidery is to make the flower a part of the body of the phoenixes or the dragons in which plants and animals were intertwined with each other realistically and fantastically.

In the history of Chinese art and crafts, the phoenix pattern ran neck and neck with the dragon pattern②. However, since the Western Zhou Dynasty,

① 战国菱格六边形纹绦，收藏于荆州博物馆，湖北江陵马山楚墓出土。几何纹样中，楚人最偏爱的是菱形纹。巧妙地利用凤的翅和尾以及花卉组成别致的菱形纹，为楚地织绣纹样所独有。

② 在中国工艺历史上，凤纹是与龙纹并驾齐驱的两大纹样，但自西周以来，凤纹在中原地区越来越少见，在楚国却越来越多，因为凤是楚人先民的图腾，在刺绣中，凤成为无可争议的主角。

the phoenix pattern had become rare in the Central Plains but more in Chu State. Because the phoenix was regarded as the totem of the Chu people, phoenixes became the undisputed protagonist in embroidery.

Patterns of Paired Dragons and Phoenixes①

① 对龙对凤纹刺绣图案(战国中期楚墓出土)

Light Yellow Fragment of Enamel Embroidered with Flying Phoenix and Floral Patterns①
(Jingzhou Museum, Unearthed from No. 1 Chu Tomb of Mashan, Jiangling)

① 战国浅黄绢刺绣飞凤花卉纹残片，荆州博物馆馆藏，湖北江陵马山一号楚墓出土。

Part of the Coverlet of the Quilt with Patterns of Dragons & Phoenixes①
(Jingzhou Museum, Unearthed from No. 1 Chu Tomb of Mashan, Jiangling)

① 蟠龙飞凤纹面衾局部，荆州博物馆馆藏，湖北江陵马山一号楚墓出土。

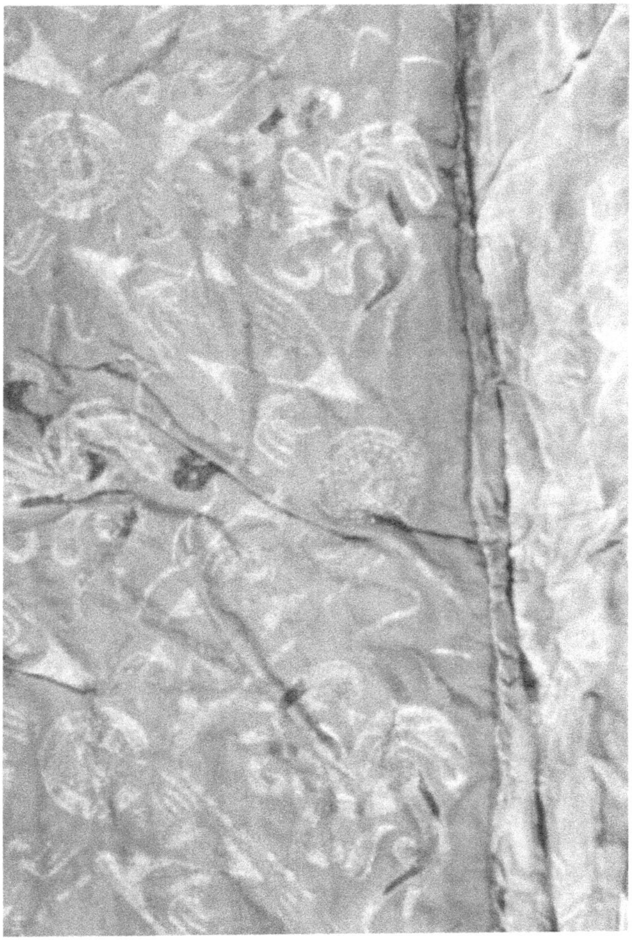

Brown Bengaline Embroidered with Golden Phoenixes①
(Jingzhou Museum, Unearthed from No. 1 Chu Tomb of Mashan, Jiangling)

This piece of Bengaline was embroidered with a flying phoenix on the red-brown mantle with the chain-stitch embroidery technique. The tall corolla, the wings, the long tail, and the flower were naturally intertwined into a gorgeous picture.

① 棕红色绢刺绣金凤鸟纹绦，荆州博物馆馆藏，湖北江陵马山一号楚墓出土。此件刺绣品在棕红色绢上以锁绣绣出一只飞步前行的凤鸟，凤鸟头部延伸出高高的花冠，双翅伸展，长尾上卷，与花卉自然地结合，构成整幅图案。

Leno Embroidered with Dragons, Phoenixes and Tigers①
(Jingzhou Museum)

① 龙凤虎纹绣罗，荆州博物馆馆藏，湖北江陵马山一号楚墓出土。

Silk Garment Replica with the Pattern of Dragons, Phoenixes, and Tigers①
(Jingzhou Museum)

On this embroidered garment, there are the embroidered patterns of a phoenix, two dragons and one tiger as a unit. The phoenix dominates the whole picture. It squats and slams on one foot. The other foot stretches forward and grabs the neck of the dragon beneath it. The dragon is escaping painfully. One wing of the phoenix hits the waist of a tiger in front. The tiger screams with large mouth in mourning; the other wing hits the waist of the dragon above. The dragon looks up and bends the neck and opens the mouth in mourning. This is a vivid picture of the phoenix battling with the dragon and the tiger.

① 湖北江陵马山一号楚墓出土的战国中期服饰实物复制品。该衣为直裾、交领右衽长衣。领、袖缘为大菱形纹锦。其衣料为罗地龙凤虎纹绣，以锁绣技法绣成。图案由龙、凤、虎缠绕穿插排列，凤鸟双翅张开，脚踏小龙；浑身布满红黑色(或灰色)条纹的斑斓猛虎，正张牙舞爪地奔向大龙，大龙作抵御状。龙凤之间相互交错、缠绕，凤的长冠与虎的长尾将纵向排列的单元联系起来，使图案的布局满而不乱，S形的曲线萦绕盘旋，显示了一种飘逸、神奇的美，充满了生机与活力，是浪漫楚风的典型代表。

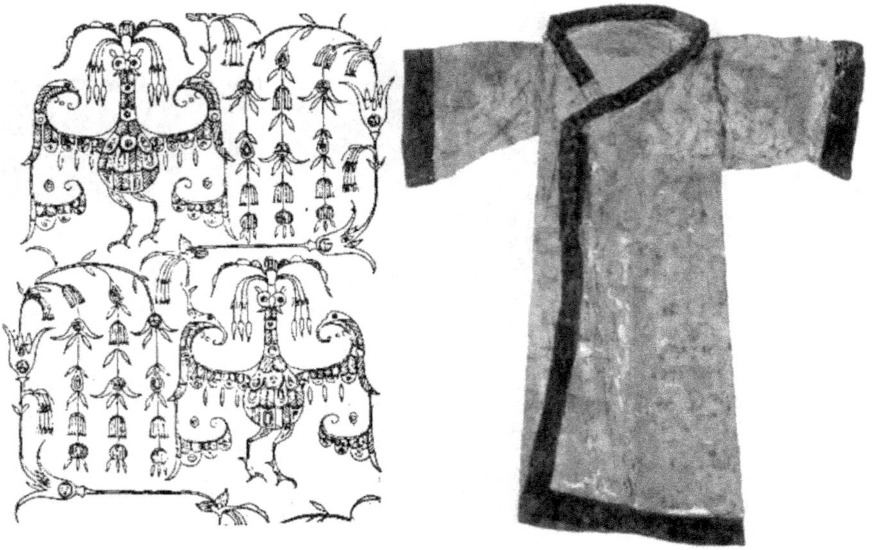

Embroidered Yellow Plain Silk Lined Robe with Three-headed Phoenixes and Floral Patterns①
(Jingzhou Museum, Unearthed from No. 1 Chu Tomb of Mashan, Jiangling)

There are three main types of character patterns in Chu embroidery: dancers, hunters and drivers. These character patterns were drawn in simple and vivid lines and the scenes of playing music, dancing and hunting into the art of embroidery. They are similar to the contemporary characters inscribed in the bronze vessels in the north.

Judged from the archaeological materials and literature, the clothing in Chu State included at least unlined robes, robes, sashes, skirts, trousers, smocks, shoes, gloves, armors and so on. Three pieces of unlined robes were unearthed from the No. 1 Tomb of Mashan, Jiangling, Hubei Province.

---

① 三头凤花卉纹绣浅黄绢绵袍，湖北江陵马山一号楚墓出土。楚绣中的人物纹样主要有三种：舞者、猎者和御者。这些人物纹样都是图案化的，手法简练，情趣横溢，把乐舞、狩猎这些生活场景引入刺绣艺术，与北方同时期的铜壶、铜鉴上的人物纹饰有异曲同工之妙。

Embroidered Purple Plain Silk Robe with Patterns of a Dragon Battling a Phoenix①
(Jingzhou Museum, Unearthed from No. 1 Chu Tomb of Mashan, Jiangling)

The robe is a kind of long and thick lined garment which the upper part was connected at the waist with the lower part. The styles of the Chu robes are all straight-front garments with right front-part overlapping the left front-part, which inherited the costumes of the Zhou Dynasty. Seven pieces of robes were unearthed from the No. 1 Chu Tomb of Mashan.

So far, the pair of brown cotton-padded plain silk leggings (绔) embroidered with phoenix and floral patterns unearthed from No. 1 Chu Tomb of Mashan in Jiangling is the only relic of this kind of clothing in the Eastern Zhou Dynasty. According to the situation unearthed at the time, it was a kind of close-fitting clothing covered with a skirt.

① 龙凤相搏纹绣紫红绢单衣。

Silk Painting Depicting Man Driving a Dragon Discovered from No. 1 Pit Zidanku Tomb in the Warring States Period in Changsha (Hunan Provincial Museum)①

---

① 人物御龙帛画是战国中晚期的帛画精品，1973 年于湖南省长沙市子弹库一号墓出土，画中楚国男子戴高冠、着曲裾深衣、佩长剑。大袖袍服，衣襟盘曲而下，形成曲裾，是典型的深衣样式。在同时期的木俑、铜人身上，也能见到同样的服饰。人物表情生动传神，服饰线条流畅舒展，恰到好处地表现了长袍的质感和动态，是中国早期肖像画的杰出代表。是中华人民共和国 2002 年公布的 64 件禁止出国(境)展览文物之一。现藏于湖南省博物馆。

The Warring States Period was the period of great ideological revolution and artistic development in the Chinese history. In the middle reaches of the Yangtze River, Chu Culture took the leading position in the field of art and technology. With its rich imagination and exquisite skills, Chu silk production and embroidery art has made outstanding contributions to the ancient silk industry in China and the world.

Chapter 6

Chu Music in Musical Instruments

In the Pre-Qin Period, ritual was the social norm for classes and ethics, and music was an important means to reflect this norm. The complicated ritual system prompted music to an unprecedented height in Chinese history and made ancient Chinese musical instruments develop to the fullest. Xunzi, a great Confucian thinker in the Warring States Period, gave the comment on the relationship of music and rite: "Music brings harmony, while rite brings reason. Music produces sympathy, while rite tempers the manners. Music and rite is concerned with head and heart."

According to *The Rites in Zhou Dynasty*, there were eight kinds of musical instruments① classified according to materials used, such as Jin (the bronze musical instrument), shi (the stone musical instrument), tu (the pottery musical instrument), ge (the leather musical instrument), si (the stringed musical instrument), pao (the gourd musical instrument), zhu (the bamboo musical instrument), and mu (the wood musical instrument).

In recent decades, more than 700 musical relics were unearthed from the

---

① 八音原为中国历史上最早的乐器科学分类法，分为金(钟、镈、铙)、石(磬)、土(埙、缶)、革(鼗、雷鼓)、丝(琴、瑟)、匏(笙、竽)、竹(箫、篪)、木(柷、敔)八类。

Chu tombs or the Chu-related tombs, and more than 300 bronze bells were excavated. The Tomb of Marquis Yi of Zeng discovered in 1978 more comprehensively reflected the level of Chu music because six categories of musical instruments were discovered there.

6. 1 Musical Instruments

The musical instrument in banquets or ceremonies were based on chime bells and chime stones accompanied with other orchestral or percussion instruments.

The musical instruments unearthed in Marquis Yi Tomb include two groups: The chime bells and chime stones accompanied by other 115 pieces of wind, string and other percussion instruments in the central chamber construct the band of the metal-and-stone music, which played the grand and noble music for ancestral sacrifice or ceremonies; while the qin and se and other instruments in the eastern chamber build a band for bedchamber music, which plays soft and gentle music for sleeping.

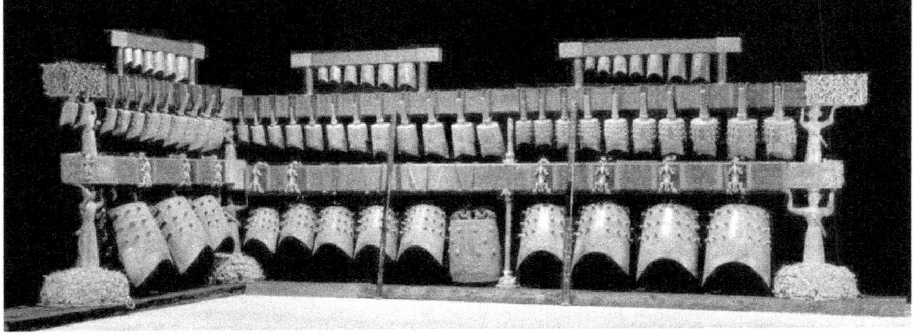

The Bronze Chime Bells of Marquis Yi's Tomb
(Hubei Provincial Museum)

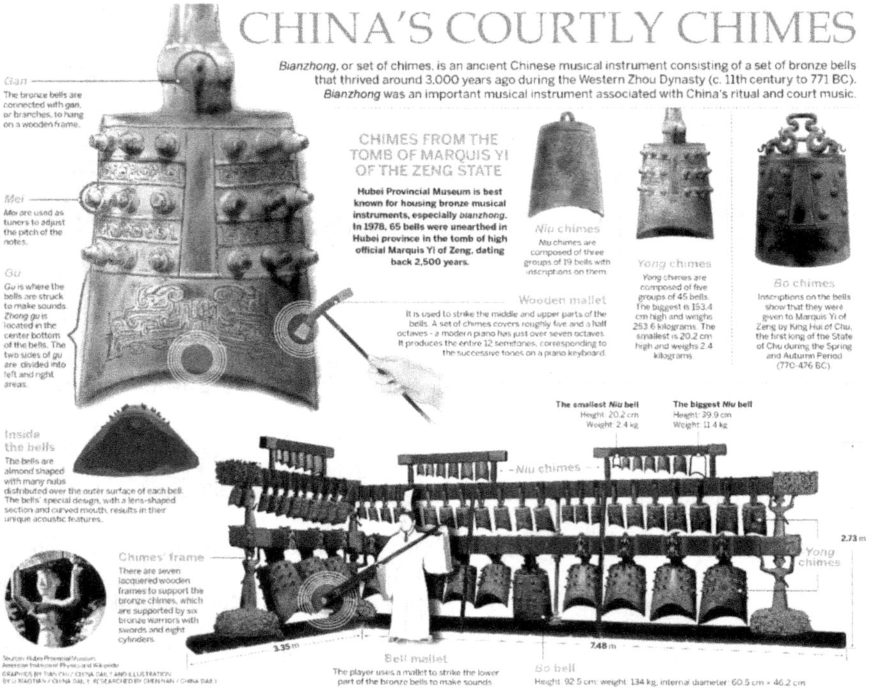

China's Courtly Chimes
(From *China Daily*, Wednesday, November 8, 2017)

Bronze chime bells are the representative of the prominent stature of ancient Chinese musical instruments production. First used in the Shang Dynasty, bronze chime bells became popular during the Western Zhou Dynasty (1046BC-771BC). In 1978, a fine set of chime bells was unearthed from the Tomb of Marquis Yi, a local lord in a state named Zeng during the Warring States Period (in present Suizhou City of Hubei Province), which epitomizes the wealth and prestige of a nobility as well as an important means to bringing about harmony in personal and social life in ancient China.

The Bronze Bo Bell of King Xiongzhang of Chu ①
(Hubei Provincial Museum)

The Bronze Bell of King Ni of Chu of the Western Zhou Dynasty ②
(Shanxi Museum)

① 曾侯乙编钟里的楚王熊章所赠镈钟。
② 西周楚公逆钟。

The Bronze Chime Bell①
(The Palace Museum)

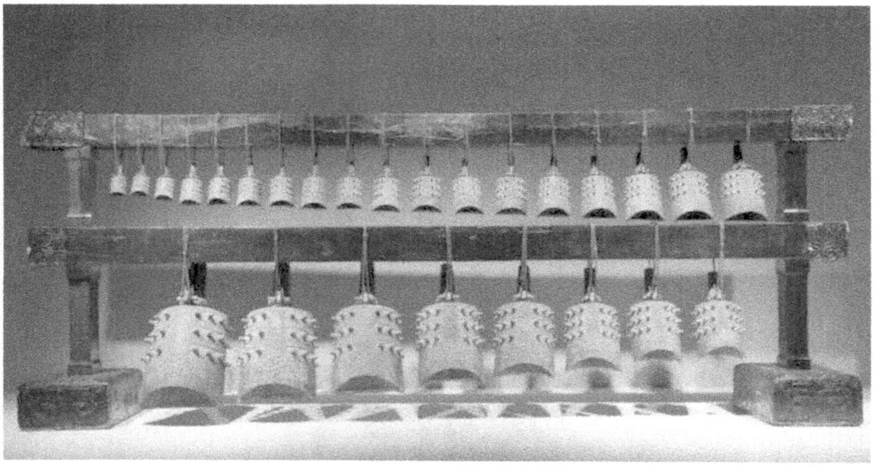

The Bronze Chime Bell of Wang Sungao②
(Henan Museum)

This set of chime bells was unearthed in the Chu tomb of Xiachuan Temple in Xichuan, Henan Province in 1978. It consists of 26 bells. It is the

① 楚国青铜编钟(战国)，1957 年河南信阳长台关楚墓出土。

② 王孙诰编钟，1978 年河南淅川下寺楚墓出土，现收藏于河南博物院，共 26 枚角钟，是我国目前发现的春秋时期数量最多、规模最大、音域最宽广、保存最完好的青铜礼乐器，为我们研究中国古音乐提供了宝贵的资料。

bronze ritual instrument with the largest number, the largest scale, the widest range of tones and the best preservation during the Spring and Autumn Period. It provides valuable information for studying Chinese ancient music.

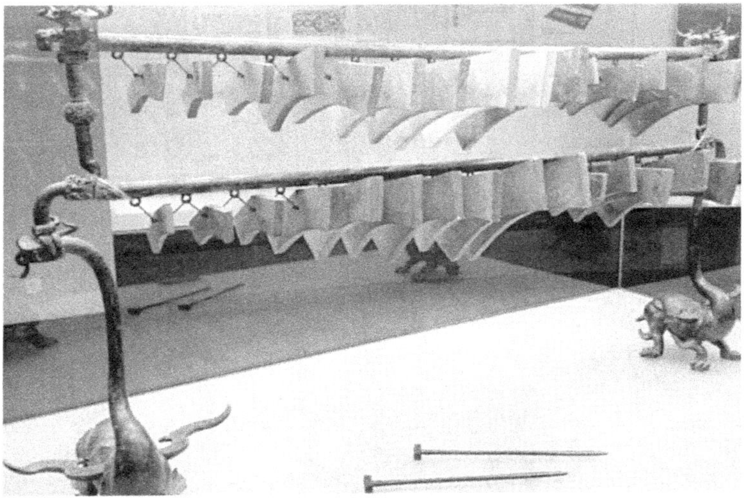

The Chime Stone of Marquis Yi of Zeng①
(Hubei Provincial Museum)

Stone refers to the musical instruments such as the stone qing (stone chime) which are made of stone or jade. As the earliest percussion, it may originate in working when ancients found the pleasing sound produced by the stone tools such as stone shovels and used them for dancing. As far as we know, the earliest ancient stone qing in the Xia Dynasty were unearthed in Shanxi in China. A piece of stone qing in the early Shang Dynasty was excavated in Erlitou Site in Yanshi of Henan Province. There are some sets of chime stone of the Shang Dynasty unearthed as well. As musical and ritual instrument, the use of chime bell and chime stone is the symbol of power and prestige of the feudal nobility.

① 曾侯乙编磬。

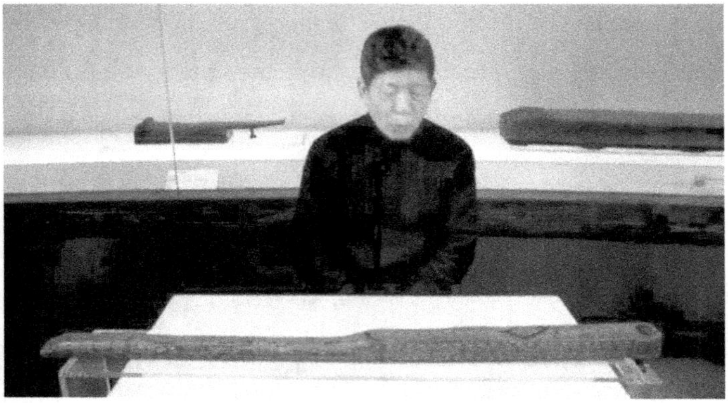

Jun Bell of Marquis Yi of Zeng①
(Hubei Provincial Museum)

The Bronze Base of Jian Drum of Marquis Yi's Tomb②
(Hubei Provincial Museum)

① 曾侯乙均钟。

② 曾侯乙墓出土的建鼓，是当时所知我国年代最早的建鼓实物，年代为战国早期。

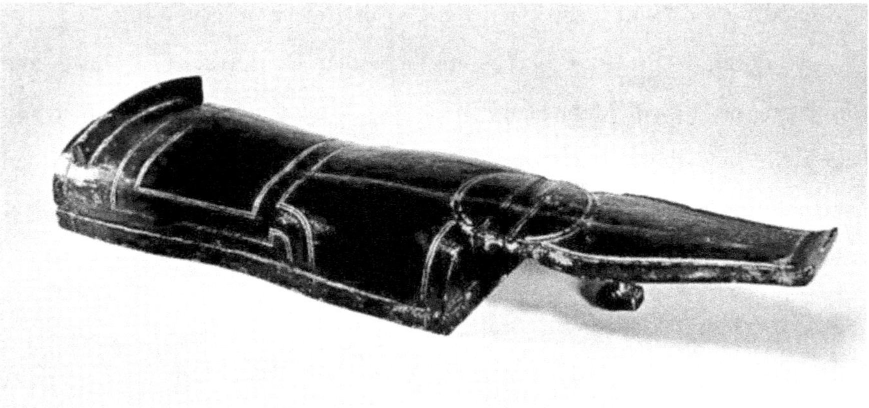

A 10-stringed Zither of Marquis Yi of Zeng①
(Hubei Provincial Museum)

Silk musical instruments are mostly stringed instruments (including those that are plucked, bowed, and struck). Since ancient times the Chinese have used silk for strings, this kind of musical instrument gets the name "silk musical instrument" though today metal or nylon are more frequently used.

As two kinds of the oldest Chinese stringed instruments, qin and se have been widely played since the Western Zhou Dynasty, while in the Eastern Zhou Dynasty they had been playing an extremely important position in the ritual in the Central Plains.

To create or enjoy a tranquil atmosphere, the ancient Chinese literati or musicians enjoyed playing or appreciating the zither by a stream, in the bamboo forest, in the mountain, in the snow or in a moonlit night. The sounds of the zither blended with the echoes of the mountains will remove the worry and burden, and make musicians and audiences get the solace and soothing, and move into a pure natural world.

There are some legendary originators of the ancient qin in China. People

① 曾侯乙十弦琴。

attributed Fu Xi, Shun, and Shen Nong to the invention of the qin.

According to Professor Li Youping in Wuhan Conservatory of Music, the first doctor of Musical Archaeology in China, "The ancient zither originates in Chu area since there is physical evidence of a number of early unearthed ancient zithers in Chu area as well as the documentary records of the ancient zither in Chu State."

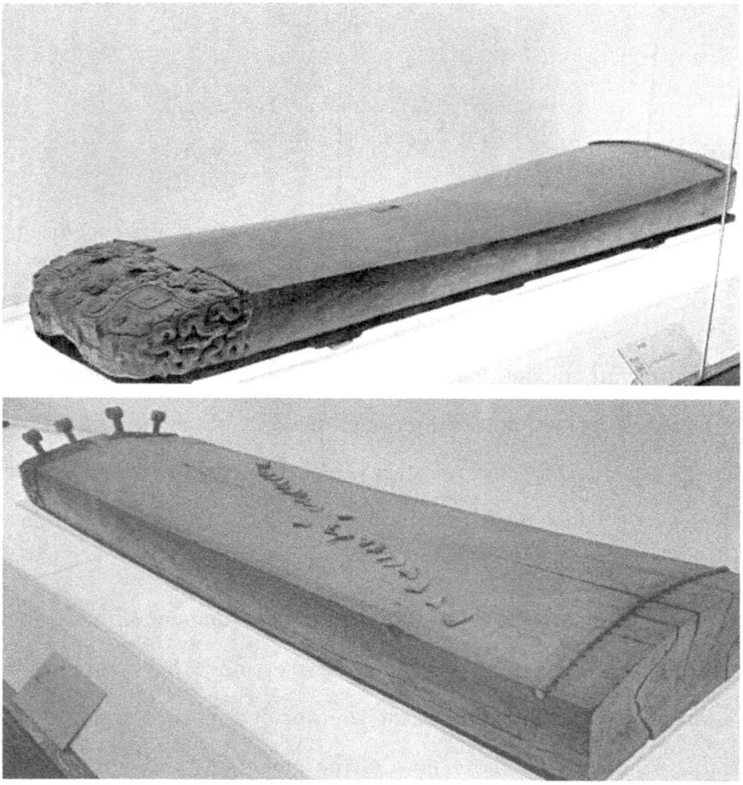

Se of Marquis Yi of Zeng①
(Hubei Provincial Museum)

① 曾侯乙墓发掘以前，湖北江陵、湖南长沙楚墓中屡有瑟出土，但曾侯乙墓出土达 12 件，且年代更早，制作更精美。

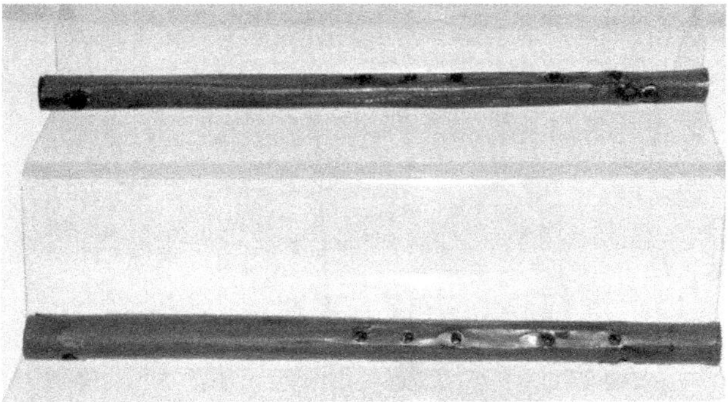

Chi of Marquis Yi of Zeng①
(Hubei Provincial Museum)

Bamboo Musical Instrument mainly refers to wind instruments, which includes all kinds of flutes, panpipes made of bamboo.

Panpipes of Marquis Yi of Zeng (the Earliest Bamboo Panpipes Found in China)②
(Hubei Provincial Museum)

① 篪，曾侯乙墓出土。

② 排箫在屈原的《九歌湘君》中称"参差"，由十三根参差不齐的竹管编连而成。排箫只在文字和汉墓石碑中见到，曾侯乙排箫出土，人们得以见到它的真面目。

The Drum with Lacquered Tiger-and-Phoenix-shaped Wooden Stand
of the Warring States Period①
(Jingzhou Museum)

The Picture of Striking the Bells on the Lacquered Mandarin
Duck-shaped Box of Marquis Yi②
(Hubei Provincial Museum)

① 战国虎坐鸟架鼓(荆州博物馆)是古代的一种乐器，与编钟、编磬组合使用，一般只出土于楚国贵族墓葬。

② 曾侯乙彩漆鸳鸯形盒上的撞钟图。

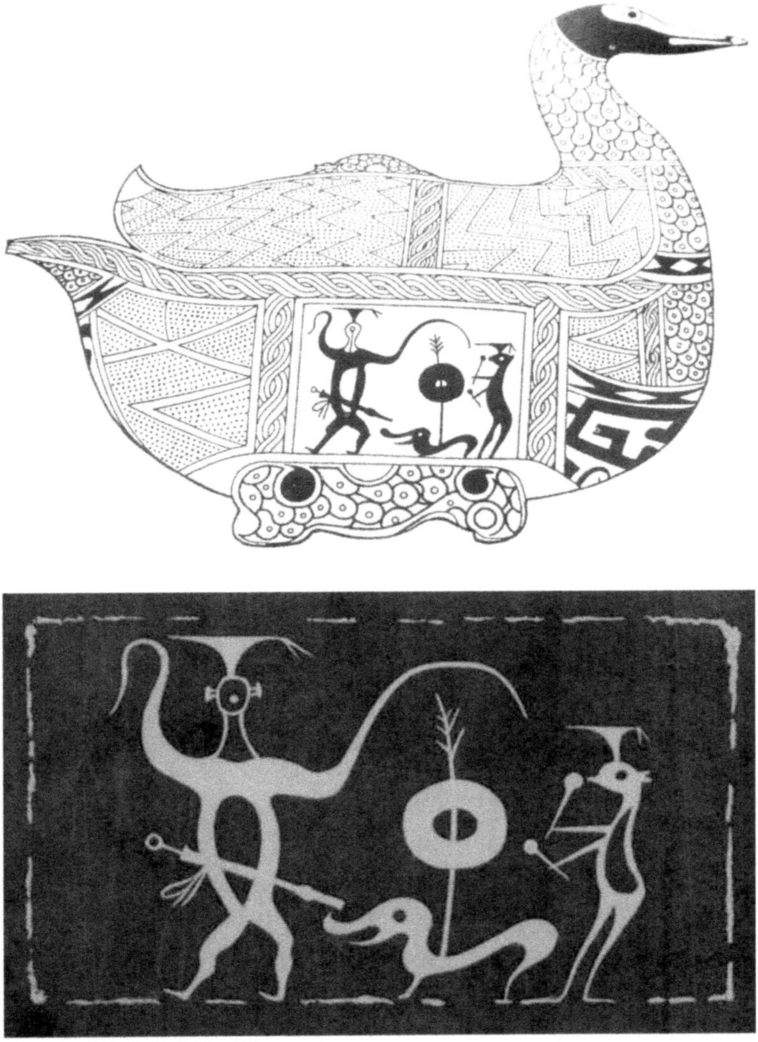

The Picture of Beating Drum & Dancing on the Lacquered Mandarin Duck-shaped Box of Marquis Yi①

① 曾侯乙彩漆鸳鸯形盒上的击鼓跳舞图。

6.2 The Story of "Yu Boya and Zhong Ziqi"

Many Chinese idioms reflect the music activities of the Chu people, "high mountains and flowing water", "too lofty to be popular" ①, "be besieged on all sides by the songs of Chu State" ②, and so on.

The idiom "lofty mountains and flowing water" is a classical allusion from the story of Yu Boya and Zhong Ziqi of the Spring and Autumn Period. Yu Boya was a famous musician at that time. One night when he was appreciating the moon and the scene on the Han River, he was touched by the bright moon and cool breeze and began to play the zither. The melody was so beautiful that a man on the bank shouted, "bravo!" There was a woodcutter standing on the bank. When Boya played a piece of music eulogizing the high mountains, the woodcutter said, "Wonderful! The melody is as magnificent and dignified as Mount Tai!" When he played a piece of music depicting the turbulent waves, the woodcutter said, "Magnificent! The melody is as vast and mighty as the great rivers!" That woodcutter was Zhong Ziqi. Since then, they became bosom friends. After Zhong Ziqi died, Yu Boya never played his zither because he thought nobody in this world understood him.

---

① 曲高和寡：出自《宋玉·答楚王问》，原意为乐曲的格调越高能跟着唱的人就越少。比喻越是艰深、高雅的东西，理解的人就越少。这个成语来自宋玉《对楚王问》，文中讲到唱通俗的《下里巴人》，在楚城中有几千人跟着唱，而唱高雅的《阳春白雪》时，跟着唱的只有几十人。后人也用"下里巴人"和"阳春白雪"指代通俗的文艺作品和高雅的文艺作品。旧指知音难得，现比喻言论或作品不通俗，能了解的人很少。

② 四面楚歌：出自《史记·项羽本纪》，楚汉战争中，项羽被刘邦围困垓下，刘邦让士兵夜夜高唱楚歌，以动摇项羽的军心。形容人们遭受各方面攻击或逼迫的人事环境，处于孤立无援、四面受敌的困境中。

Guqintai (Photo by Shi Yaochen)

Guqintai① was first built in the Northern Song Dynasty. It is located at the foot of Guishan Mountain and on the shore of Yuehu Lake in Wuhan City. With the Yellow Crane Tower and the Qingchuan Pavilion, Guqintai is one of the most famous scenic spots in Wuhan. It is also the most famous music relic in China and one of the key protection unit of cultural relics in Hubei Province.

---

① "天下知音第一台"古琴台，又名俞伯牙台，始建于北宋时期。位于湖北省武汉市汉阳区龟山脚下，月湖之滨，连接武汉长江大桥和江汉一桥；东对龟山、北临月湖，湖景相映，景色秀丽，幽静宜人，文化内涵丰富，构成一个广阔深远的艺术境界。它与"天下江山第一楼"——黄鹤楼、"楚国晴川第一楼"——晴川阁并称为武汉三大名胜，是荆楚大地著名的风景旅游胜地，中国最著名的音乐文化古迹，也是湖北省、武汉市重点文物保护单位之一。古琴台建筑群占地约 15 亩，除殿堂主建筑外，还有庭院、林园、花坛、茶室等，规模虽然不大，但布局精巧、层次分明。殿堂前有琴台，为汉白玉筑成的方形石台，约 20 平方米，相传为伯牙抚琴之处。清朝嘉庆初年，湖广总督毕沅主持重建古琴台，请汪中代笔撰《琴台之铭并序》(一说为《汉上琴台之铭并序》)和《伯牙事考》。光绪十年(公元 1884 年)，黄彭年撰《重修汉阳琴台记》。光绪十六年(公元 1890 年)，杨守敬主持并亲自书丹，将《琴台之铭并序》《伯牙事考》《重修汉阳琴台记》重镌立于琴台碑廊之中，并书"古琴台"三字刻于大门门楣。

This story was recorded in the *Works of Lie Zi*. From this story, people have derived the idiom "high mountain and running water" to refer to understanding and appreciative friends. It also refers to the harsh reality that talented people can rarely meet those who can really appreciate them.

There are three Chu music officials recorded with the surname "Zhong" in the literature. Whether Zhong Ziqi once served as the official of music was unknown, but his profound musical accomplishment showed that he was probably a secluded music official.

Chapter 7

Chu Trade and Law in Objects

Trade and law are another important aspects for us to learn about Chu Culture.

7.1 Chu Trade

Trade, or more broadly, exchange, has always been a driving force of

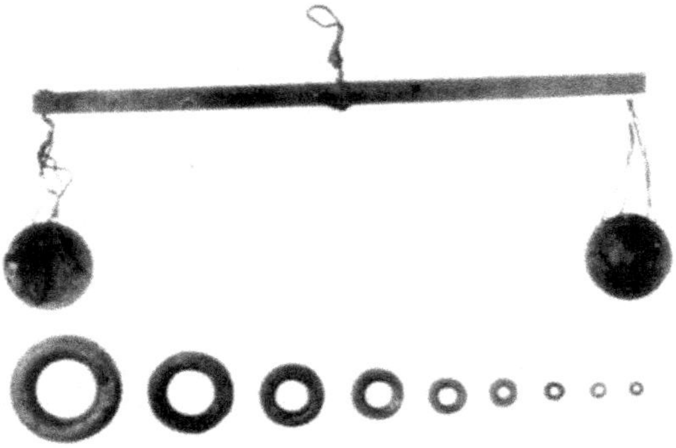

Balance and Weight①
Unearthed from the Chu Tomb of the Warring States Period in Zuojiagong Mountain in Changsha
(Hunan Provincial Museum)

① 1954年长沙左家公山战国晚期楚墓出土了铜砝码、天平等。天平保存很完整，木杆长27厘米，中间置丝线提纽，两端各系一铜盘。出土砝码大小共九个，其中最大的重四市两，此外的依次递减，重量各相差一半，制作非常规范，是当时称量金币的科学衡器。

society. Trade was a primary force behind Chu expansion. Chu State, located both north and south of the Yangtze River, sat on an interface between the south and the Central Plains. The traders from Chu served as intermediaries in facilitating the movement of desired exotic products from western and southern frontier regions to the north.

The Bronze Weight with Inscription of "Jun Yi"①
Unearthed from the Chu Tomb of the Warring States Period in
Zuojiagong Mountain in Changsha
(Hunan Provincial Museum)

Chu merchants and rulers focused their interests on three regions: the Southwest, the Jiangnan, and the Lingnan regions.

The Southwest includes the modern provinces of Sichuan, Yunnan, Guizhou, and Western Guangxi. It is hilly and dominated by the Yunnan-Guizhou plateau sweeping down from Tibet. The relationship and contact between Chu and Ba—the principal ethnic group/state of the Southwest—was undoubtedly primarily motivated by trade. According to the *Huayang Guozhi*, Ba was a source for silk, hemp, fish, salt, copper, iron, cinnabar, lacquer,

① "钧益"铜砝码，1954 年长沙左家公山战国楚墓出土。"钧益"铜砝码是目前所见楚国天平砝码中最完整的一套，是研究楚国权衡制度以及权衡史的重要资料。

tea and honey. A passage in *The Hanfeizi*(*Han Fei Zi*) states that "raw gold was found in the lands south of Jing (Chu)", in which "the lands south of Jing" may refer to the Mei River region (today's Jinsha Jiang, Golden Sands River) the western part of the Yangtze River that forms the southern border of Sichuan with Yunnan.

The Jiangnan region includes the modern provinces of Hunan, Jiangxi, Zhejiang, and Fujian. Although hilly as well, this region is endowed with fertile river valleys. Both temperate and subtropical, this region served as a transition zone for Chinese expansion on its way to the truly tropical Lingnan region as well as the resource of gold, copper, tin and other mines.

Lingnan encompasses the modern provinces of Guangdong and Eastern Guangxi and continues into Northern Vietnam. This region was famous for its exotic products such as kingfisher feathers, pearls, tortoise, aromatic and medicinal plants, and fragrant barks and resins. During the Han Dynasty, Panyu, located near today's Guangzhou, was already an established trading center distributing tropical products. *The Shiji* stated that "Panyu is the most important city in the area, being the center for pearls, rhinoceros horn, tortoise shell, fruit, and cloth." The "Treatise on Geography" (*Di Li Zhi*) of *The Han Shu* mentioned the Hepu district, located on the coast of Guangxi Province, which bounded with rhinoceros, elephants, tortoise shell, pearls, silver, copper, and fruit. Hainan Island, known then as Zhuhai (Shore of Pearls), was visited and even colonized by the Han Dynasty in order to secure access to its medicinal products, pearls, tortoise shell, ivory, and colorful or scented woods. Chu pearls were most likely from the tropical waters of the Hepu district along the coast of Guangxi and Hainan Island.

7. 1. 1 Archaeological Objects in Chu Trade

There is archaeological evidence for activities of Chu trade and exchange over a wide territory extending from Henan and Hubei provinces in the north, to Jiangsu in the east, to Sichuan in the west and down into Hunan, Guangxi, and Guangdong in the south.

In 1957 archaeologists discovered a pair of bronze bamboo-shaped objects from the site of Qiujia Huayuan, Shou County of Anhui Province. Archaeologists believed that these two objects called "E Jun Tallies" functioned as a kind of permit issued to authorize the holder to trade in a designated area. E Jun, or Prince E, the name of the specific individual mentioned in these inscriptions, is thought to have been a son or brother of King Huai of Chu (328BC-298BC). These gold-inlaid "land route tally" and "water route tally" are precious objects in studying the transportation, commerce, taxes, geography, rules of using tallies, the king's rights and duties, and the relationship between the king and the prince.

The E Jun Qi Tally ①
(Anhui Provincial Museum)

In 1957 archaeologists unearthed a pair of bronze bamboo-shaped tallies from the site of Qiujia Huayuan of Shou County, Anhui. These two objects functioned as a kind of permit issued to E Jun or Prince E, authorizing him to trade in a designated area. According to the inscription on the tallies, Prince E had been giving special trading privileges by the King of Huai of Chu State (328BC-298 BC). They exempted him from paying taxes and limited his traveling time and routes by water or land as well as the amount of goods in quantity and type. The water route was outlined from Echeng along the Yangtze River to the Dongting Lake along the Xiang River, and terminally to Ying by water and the land route was from Echeng to Ying.

① 鄂君启铜节(安徽省博物馆馆藏)，战国时期青铜器物，1957 年安徽省寿县城东丘家花园出土。节是古时由帝王或政府颁发的用于水陆交通的凭证，有虎形、马形、龙形、竹节形等。鄂君启节是公元前 323 年楚怀王颁发给鄂君启的经商、运输货物免税凭证，共出土 5 件，舟节 2 件，车节 3 件，合在一起呈圆筒状。"鄂君启"中的"鄂"为地名(今湖北省鄂州市)，"启"是鄂君之名。铜节分舟节和车节两种，用时双方各持一半，合节验证无讹才发生效力。铭文中详细规定了鄂君启水路、陆路交通运输的路线、车船大小与数量、运载额、运输货物的种类、禁运货物和纳税及免税情况等。是研究战国时楚国符节制度、商业、交通、地理和赋税制度的珍贵资料和实物证据。节面阴刻错金铭文，在金文中别具一格。郭沫若先生曾以鄂君启节为例，说明错金铭文在战国时期达到了前所未有的高度。

Yanke Copper Measuring Cup①
(Hunan Provincial Museum)

Yanke copper is a standard instrument for measuring in Chu State. The content of the inscription relates to tax collection and salary payment, which is highly valued by the government. There are many pieces of copper measuring cups unearthed in Chu State. Judged from the inscriptions, this copper cup is the most precious. The inscriptions on this cup recorded the ambassador of Yan State made an inquiry from the King of Chu, which was not recorded in the history book. The "Luo" in the inscription is the county magistrate of Chu State, and it is the predecessor of the ancient city of Miluo of Hunan.

① 燕客铜量(湖南省博物馆馆藏)。燕客铜量是楚国一种量器的标准器。铭文内容涉及赋税征收、俸禄发放等，备受政府的重视。楚国铜量发现多件，无论是从文字的多少还是所记载的内容来看，此铜量最为珍贵。铜量所记燕国使者询问楚王的事件史书上没有记载。铭文中的"罗"为楚国的县邑，为今湖南古汨罗城的前身。

7. 1. 2　Chu Currency in Trade

Bronze Cowry-shaped "Ant-nose" Coins①
(Hubei Provincial Museum)

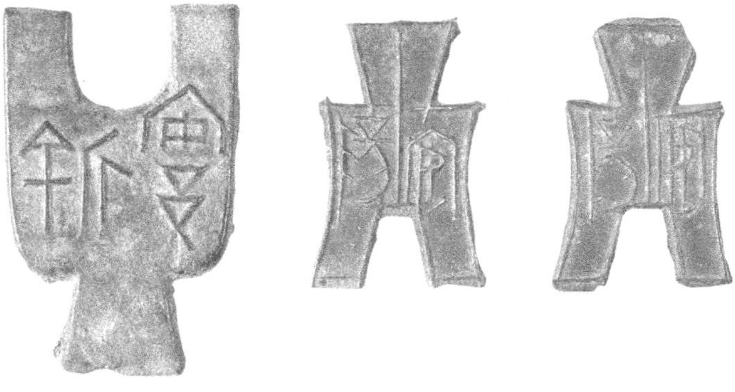

Spade-shaped Coin②
(Hubei Provincial Museum)

① 战国蚁鼻钱，1963 年孝感野猪湖出土。

② 布币，战国安邑釿布、安阳布。

Gold is another evidence for the trade in Chu State.

According to *Zhanguoce*, "Gold, pearls, gems, rhinoceros horn and ivory all come from Chu." In *Shiji*, the chapter of "Biographies of the Money-makers" recorded that gold came from Yuzhang and bamboo from Changsha."

Although Chu ritual vessels were generally not made of gold, many Chu bronze vessels were inlaid with complex designs made from gold and silver or covered with gold leaf. Its currency, named Ying-yuan, was minted from gold. The quest for gold sources to maintain a steady supply both for use and trade was doubtlessly one reason for Chu expansion into lands to the south and southwest.

Ying-yuan was the earliest original gold coin in ancient China. "Ying" is the name of the capital city of Chu State and "Yuan" is the weight unit of currency. When in use, the gold plate or gold cake was cut into pieces and weighed as needed. Gold Ying-yuan has very important historical and cultural values. Most of gold "Ying-yuan" were unearthed in Jingzhou, Hubei Province, indicating that Jingzhou is of profound significance for the study of Chu Culture.

Ying-yuan of Chu State①
(Shou County Museum)

① 楚国郢爰。

Ying-yuan of Chu State
(Henan Provincial Musem)

7.1.3 The Southern Silk Road

According to the documents, there was a mysterious general named Zhuang Qiao① who rebelled and invaded Dian State during the period of King Huai and King Qingxiang's reign. Zhuang Qiao took an ancient road which ran across Yun-Gui Plateau from the Capital of Ying in the East to the Capital of Huashicheng (present Patana City in India) in the West. That road began at the middle reaches of the Yangtze River in China and ended at the middle reaches of the Ganges River in India. This is a Southern Silk Road, which is about 200 years earlier than the Northern Silk Road②.

There are two evidences for this ancient Southern Silk Road. One is the scattering of the dragonfly-eyed glass beads, and the other is the book of

① 庄蹻入滇。
② 张正明,《楚史》, 湖北教育出版社, 1995, p. 344。

Zheng Lun (*Political Essays*) by Shang Nayan①, a minister of Mogato Kingdom in Peacock Dynasty, in which Shang Nayan mentioned the silk from China.

In terms of Zhang Zengqi,② the dragonfly-eyed glass beads discovered in Yunnan were first imported from South Asia by way of West Asia during the Spring and Autumn Period and the Warring States Period. For example, the glass beads from No. 1 Tomb of Hou Gu Dui were the artifacts in the late Warring States Period. Therefore, the Southern Silk Road maybe existed during the Spring and Autumn Period and the Warring States Period.

Dragonfly-eyed Beads from Tomb of Marquis Yi of Zeng③
(Hubei Provincial Museum)

Dragonfly-eye-shaped glass beads discovered from the Chu tombs and

① 公元前320—315年，摩揭陀王国孔雀王朝的大臣商那阎著有《政论》一书，说到从中国运去的丝。

② 张增祺，战国至西汉时期滇池区域发现的西亚文物，《思想战线》，1982年第2期。

③ 1978年，湖北随州曾侯乙墓出土了173颗表面布满圆圈纹的琉璃佩珠，被称为“蜻蜓眼”。这些“蜻蜓眼”式玻璃珠据材料成分分析，应来自西亚或南亚。

Zeng tombs of the Warring States in Hubei and Hunan provinces are completely different from the traditional Chinese decorative style but similar with those in West Asia and South Asia.

Dragonfly-eyed Glass Beads and Tube①
(Hunan Provincial Museum)

So far, these glass beads are the only evidence of cultural exchanges between Chinese and foreign countries in the Pre-Qin Dynasty.

7.2 Chu Law in Bamboo Slips

The books transmitted to modern readers from early China, whether histories, philosophical works, or anthologies, do not tell us much about the practical operation of legal institutions. In the last few decades the excavation of some ancient graves containing thousands of strips of legal and ritual texts begins to fill the gaps in understanding the law in ancient China. Several great "law graves" have been found in the heartland of cultural Chu.

In April 1986 a team of archaeologists working on the construction of the new Jingmen-Shashi railroad investigated a small group of Chu tombs on a hill named Baoshan in Jingmen, Hubei Province. Tomb 2, the largest of the group of five Baoshan graves, yielded 278 well-preserved inscribed bamboo

① 战国蜻蜓眼玻璃珠和管，1975 年于湖南湘乡市牛形山一号战国楚墓出土。

strips, containing 12, 472 graphs. These graphs tell us that the master of this tomb was a high official, the Zuoyin Shao Tuo, a minister of the Chu judicial system.

These documents offer legal historians an irreplaceable glimpse of the actual operation of Chu law in the Warring States Period.

The Excavation Spot of Baoshan Tomb 2, Jingmen Hubei

The burial pit of Tomb 2 is 34. 4 by 31. 9 meters in size. The wooden structure of the first guo was built resting on the bottom of the tomb over a small "waist pit", in which was buried a goat, together with wool and silk textiles. Like a wooden house, the first guo contained not only a central chamber, in which the grave master's body within an inner guo and three nested guan (coffins), but also four surrounding chambers. The rich furnishings of these chambers hinted Shao Tuo's privileged life aboveground and the wish to continue to enjoy a comfortable existence underground afterlife. Ritual and dining vessels were found in the east chamber; weapons and horse and chariot gear in the south; an intricately built folding bed, bamboo containers and other items needed for traveling, as well as a bundle of blank bamboo strips in the west chamber, and pillows, bamboo mats, boxes, and other comforts of daily life, together with two groups of inscribed bamboo strips, a scraping knife for erasing scribal mistakes, and a hair writing brush, in the north chamber.

The Bamboo Strips of Legal Documents from Tomb 2 at Baoshan①
(Hubei Provincial Museum)

These bamboo slips were unearthed in No. 2 Chu Tomb of the Warring States Period in Baoshan, Jingmen in 1987. There are 278 bamboo slips and one bamboo rafts including grave inventory lists, divination strips, and legal or administrative documents. These bamboo slips include the dates in the form of year, month and day. They provide valuable information for studying the political, economic, legal and historical geography of Chu State and other countries during the Warring States Period and the Qin and Han dynasties, as well as the study of calligraphy. Most of the Chu Bamboo Slips are written in seal script with the clerical script, from which we can see the evolution of seal script to clerical script.

① 包山楚简，1987年出土于湖北省荆门市包山二号战国楚墓。共计有278枚竹简和1枚竹牍，包括司法文书简、卜筮祭祷简和遣策三种。这些竹简内容丰富，纪年明确，对研究战国时期楚国和其他列国，秦、汉时期的政治、经济、法律和历史地理，以及文字、书法研究等提供了十分珍贵的资料。楚简大多篆体结字以隶行出之，由此可见由篆变隶的轨迹。

Chapter 8

Chu Philosophy

The philosophy of Chu is mainly expressed in the Taoist doctrine. It is distinguished from the Confucian and Legalists in the north by the ideas of "The law of Dao is its being what it is"①, "Stillness and non-action" and "The soft overcomes the hard"②. It is also different from the later Buddhism.

8.1 Laozi

Laozi lived first in Ku County of Chen State and later in Chu State in the Late Spring and Autumn and the Early Warring States periods. Laozi was the official which is equivalent to the director of the national library or archives of the Zhou Dynasty. Laozi founded the Taoist doctrine in the south when Confucius founded the Confucian doctrine in the north.

In October 1993, a total of 804 pieces of bamboo slips were excavated from M1 Chu Tomb in the Guodian Village of Jingmen City, Hubei Province. The bamboo slips fall into three main categories: 3 works of the Taoist school, 12 Confucian works, and the documents lost before the Qin Dynasty. These bamboo

---

① 道法自然。源自：James Legge 译，《道德经》(*Tao Te Ching*)，中州古籍出版社，2016，p. 35。

② 清静无为，柔之胜刚。

The Statue of Laozi in the East Lake of Wuhan

It is said that in the 23rd year of King Zhao of Zhou, Laozi was disappointed with the decaying of the Zhou Dynasty that he left Luoyang from the Pass of Hangu riding a black buffalo. Yin Xi, the official of the Hangu Pass, admired Laozi's learning and asked him to write something down before he left. Laozi agreed to his request and wrote a book of *Tao Te Ching* (also known as *Laozi*). After finishing this book, Laozi rode his beloved buffalo westward. Since then on, nobody knows where he has gone.

The Terrace Where Laozi Ascended to Heaven①

This scenic spot is located in the hometown of Laozi in the northeast of Luyi County, Henan Province. According to the legend, Laozi ascended to heaven here.

The Stone Statue of Laozi②

(Located in Qingyuanshan Scenic Spot in Quanzhou Fujian)

① 老子升仙台，位于老子故里河南省鹿邑县城。相传老子修道成仙于此处。

② 老君造像，福建省泉州市丰泽区清源山风景名胜区主景区。

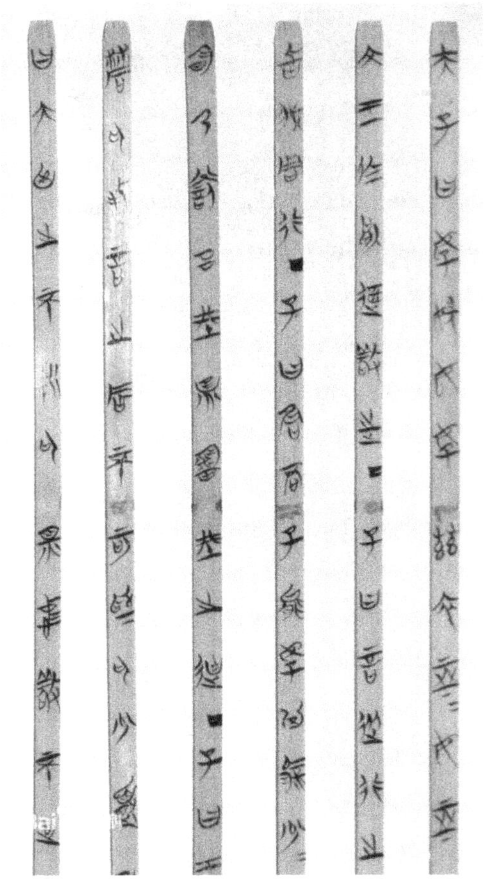

The Bamboo Slips from Chu Tomb in Guodian①
(Hubei Provincial Museum)

① 郭店楚简。1993年10月，在湖北省荆门市郭店村郭店一号楚墓发掘出竹简804枚。其中有字简730枚，共计13000多个楚国文字。楚简包含多种古籍，其中三种是道家学派的著作，其余多为儒家学派的著作，所记载的文献大多为首次发现，被鉴定为国家一级文物。郭店楚简包括十六篇先秦时期的文献，其中道家典籍三篇，分别为《老子》(甲、乙、丙)、《太一生水》、《语丛四》(《说之道》)；儒家典籍为十二篇。这批典籍除《老子》、《缁衣》见诸传世本，《五行》见于长沙马王堆出土的帛书外，其余皆为两千多年前的先秦佚籍。简本《老子》(甲、乙、丙)是20世纪90年代所见年代最早的《老子》传抄本。郭店楚简的文字是典型的楚国文字，具有楚系文字的特点，而且字体典雅、秀丽，是当时的书法精品。郭店楚简的发现，对于研究中国哲学、思想史、古文字学、简册制度和书法艺术等方面，都提供了宝贵的资料。

slips provide valuable information for the study of Chinese philosophy, the history of ancient Chinese thoughts, ancient philology, bookkeeping system and calligraphy. Three Taoist classics include *Laozi* (A, B, C), *Tai Yi Sheng Shui*, and *Yu Cong Si* (*The Way to Say*).

The most outstanding contribution of Laozi is that he established the philosophical category with the highest "Tao" and expounded the universe with Tao as the ontology, and put the philosophical concept of "Tao" above the "heaven" of religious theology. Therefore, Laozi abandoned the traditional concept of "destiny", and separated philosophy from religious theology, which opened the prelude to the independent development of Chinese philosophy①.

In view of Laozi, there are two different kinds of "Tao", one is not the enduring and unchanging "Tao" that can be named and trodden, the other is enduring and unchanging "Tao" (the nature of the universe) that cannot be named and understood②.

In Laozi's opinion, "Tao", this ontological concept first proposed in the history of Chinese philosophy, has produced everything and perfected everything in the universe, that is, "The Dao produced One; Once produced Two; Two produced Three; Three produced All things."③. Laozi first described the ontology with a negative concept, that is, "existence sprang from it as non-existent (and not named)"④. Taking the non-existence as the

① 《老子》最突出的贡献就是确立了"道"为最高的哲学范畴，阐述了以"道"为本体的宇宙生存论，将哲学概念的"道"凌驾到宗教神学的"天"之上，扬弃了"天命"等传统概念，使哲学从宗教神学中分离出来，揭开了中国哲学独立发展的序幕。

② 老子认为，生活中存在两种不同性质的道：一是可以言说的具体事物规律，即可道的"非常道"；二是不可言说的宇宙规律，即不可道的"常道"，指宇宙根本。

③ "道生一，一生二，二生三，三生万物"，源自：James Legge 译，《道德经》(*Tao Te Ching*)，中州古籍出版社，2016，p. 62。

④ "有生于无"，源自：James Legge 译，《道德经》(*Tao Te Ching*)，中州古籍出版社，2016，p. 60。

ontology is a great progress in the history of human understanding.①

Another notable feature of Laozi's philosophy is dialectics. He believed that "Non-existence lives with existence, while easiness goes side with difficulty", "Misery! Happiness is to be found by its side! Happiness! Misery lurks beneath it"②. He emphasized that the two opposite sides of things are related to each other and transform each other.③

8.2 Zhuangzi

① 这一中国哲学史上首次提出的本体论概念"道"，产生了天地万物并完善天地万物，即"道生一，一生二，二生三，三生万物"。老子还第一个用否定性的概念描述宇宙本体，即"有生于无"。以无为本体，是人类认识史上的一大进步。源自：王生铁，《楚文化概要》，湖北人民出版社，2013，pp. 231-232。

② "祸兮福之所倚，福兮祸之所伏"，源自：James Legge 译，《道德经》(*Tao Te Ching*)，中州古籍出版社，2016，p. 87。

③ 老子哲学的另一显著特色是辩证法。他认为"有无相生，难易相成"，"祸兮福之所倚，福兮祸之所伏"，主张事物的两个方面互有联系，互相转化。源自：王生铁，《楚文化概要》，湖北人民出版社，2013，pp. 231-232。

The Statue of Pengkun on Cherry Blossom Avenue in Wuhan University①

① 武汉大学樱花大道上的鹏鲲雕像及摘自《逍遥游》文字。《逍遥游》中原文为："北冥有鱼，其名曰鲲。鲲之大，不知其几千里也。化而为鸟，其名而鹏，鹏之背，不知其几千里也；怒而飞，其翼若垂天之云。"In the northern ocean there is a fish, called the k'un, I do not know how many thousand li in size. This k'un changes into a bird, called the p'eng. Its back is I do not know how many thousand li in breadth. When it is moved, it flies, its wings obscuring the sky like clouds.（林语堂 译）

Different from Laozi, Zhuangzi used rich imagination and colorful rhetoric to describe abstract attributes of "Tao" and make "Tao" vivid and down to the characteristic of "Tao"— "Ben Gen" (nature or source). With the same concept of materialism as Laozi, Zhuangzi further established the highest position of "Tao" as the ontology of the universe.

Zhuangzi focused on the way people live and the meaning people live for, and committed to elucidating the philosophy that Laozi or the Pre-Qin philosophers did not cover or pay attention to. Zhuangzi thought everything in the world was related. Big or small, happy or unhappy, useful or useless, they are all relative. If they are measured from different angles, different conclusions can be drawn.

Zhuangzi first suggested a saint to be "sageliness within and kingliness without", that is, "in his inner sageliness, he accomplishes spiritual cultivation; in his kingliness without, he functions in society"①.

The thoughts of Laozi, Zhuangzi, Confucius, and Mengzi formed the source of Chinese spiritual culture.

8. 3 Chu Philosophy in *Tai Yi Sheng Shui*

The innovation of the philosophical thoughts in Chu State is also reflected in another philosophical work "*Tai Yi Sheng Shui*" (*Taiyi Produce Water*), a thought by the legendary Chu official Guanyin, who deducted a new source of the cosmology and a new theory of creation. In this theory, "Taiyi generates water and water returns to Taiyi, which creates the sky. The sky returns to Taiji, which produces the earth." This Taoist theory is totally different from the Confucian theory of "Taiji generates two forces; two forces generate four

① 冯友兰译注。庄子最早提出的"内圣外王"思想对儒家影响深远。

quadrants; and four quadrants generate eight trigrams." Compared with this Confucian theory, *Tai Yi Sheng Shui* is much more practical and scientific①.

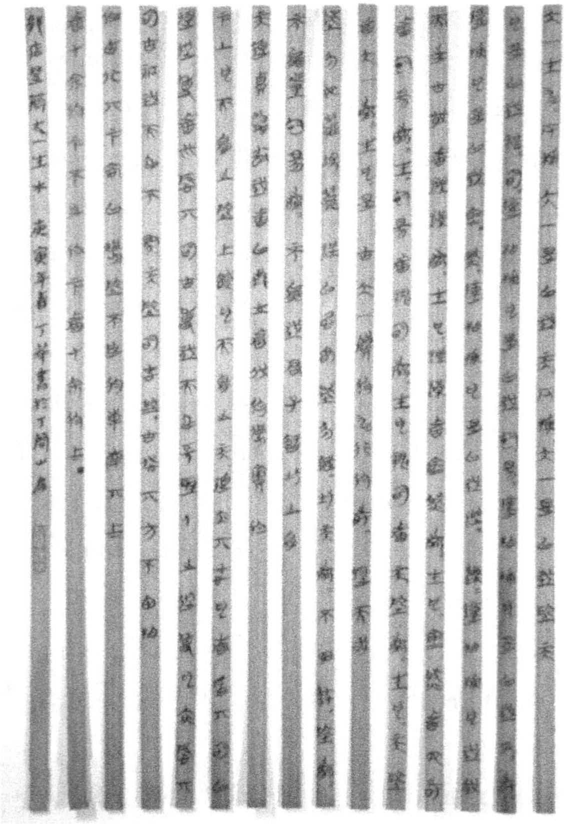

The Bamboo Slips of *Tai Yi Sheng Shui* from Guodian Chu Tomb
(Hubei Provincial Museum)

The Taoist thoughts have had far-reaching effects on the philosophy, literature, and social life of the Chinese people.

① 王生铁,《楚文化概要》, 湖北人民出版社, 2013, p. 232。

Chapter 9

Chu Literature

Chinese poetry flows from two sources. One is *Shi Jing* (*The Book of Odes/Classic of Poetry*) , the simple, moderate voice of the Northern Central Plains. The other is *Chu Ci* (*The Songs of Chu*) , the complex, lachrymose voice of the " barbarian " south. Although tradition canonized the first anthology, it is the second that had the greater influence during the formative period of the literature of the imperial age①.

9.1 Chu Literature in Qu Yuan

In the Western Han Dynasty, Liu Xiang edited Qu Yuan's 25 articles works. In the Eastern Han Dynasty Bangu recorded 25 works by Qu Yuan in *Han Shu—Yi Wen Zhi*. Wang Yi collected 25 works by Qu Yuan in his *Chu Ci Zhang Ju*(*Songs of Chu*). By now, *Li Sao*, *Jiu Ge*, *Jiu Zhang* and *Tian Wen* have been considered to be Qu Yuan's works②.

Qu Yuan created an extraordinarily new literary form from rhetoric to

① Gopal Sukhu. Monkeys, Shamans, Emperors, and Poets, from *Defining Chu*, University of Hawaii Press, 1999, p. 145.

② 西汉刘向编辑屈原作品共 25 篇，东汉班固在《汉书・艺文志》记载屈原作品也是 25 篇。王逸作《楚辞章句》录取屈原作品也是 25 篇。《离骚》《九歌》《九章》《天问》被认为是屈原作品。

content on the basis of the folk songs of the North and the South. *Li Sao*, *Jiu Ge*, *Jiu Zhang* are the insurmountable peak of lyric poetry for the following generations.

The Statue of Qu Yuan

To commemorate the famous patriotic poet Qu Yuan, Xing Yin (Wandering and Chanting) ① Pavilion and the Statue of Qu Yuan were built in the East Lake of Wuhan in 1955. On this three tiered pavilion, there is a tablet of "Xing Yin Ge" written by Guo Moruo, a famous historian and poet in China, to commemorate Qu Yuan who once wandered and chanted his poems before he drowned himself in the Mi Luo River after Chu State was conquered by Qin State during his exile.

It is evident that Qu Yuan was a great Shaman who knew all the mythical stories and excelled in witchcraft according to his *Li Sao*. Different from other Shamans in Chu State, Qu Yuan integrated witchcraft with Taoism and

① "行吟"取自《楚辞·渔父》中"至于江滨，披发行吟泽畔"。

created his Saoism①, which made his poetry filled with weirdness, mysteriousness and nobleness. The romanticism in Qu Yuan's works is neither the reverse of classicism nor the Western Romanticism. It is something miraculous, extraordinary, troubling and new, which led to the imagination along unsuspected ways to the discovery of new mysteries②.

The Bronze Statue of Qu Yuan in Qu Yuan Memorial Hall in Zigui County

① 张正明:"楚国本来只有巫学,自从楚文化进入鼎盛期后,巫学开始分流:因循者为巫学;理性化者为道学;感性化者为骚学。"

② 张正明,《楚史》,湖北教育出版社,1995,p.338。

The Bronze Statue of Qu Yuan
(In front of the New Qu Yuan Memorial Hall in Fenghuang Mountain)

Sacrificial Hall for Qu Yuan①

① 屈原祠整体建筑面积1651平方米，单檐硬山顶砖木结构，三间三进，整个建筑具有典型的江南古建筑风格。屈原祠始建于唐元和十五年(820年)，北宋改名为清烈公祠，元、明、清时曾多次修缮，才得以保存。1976年，长江葛洲坝水利工程兴建，清烈公祠由秭归县人民政府将其迁往距县城3公里的向家坪，更名为屈原祠。2006年，三峡工程蓄水，屈原祠再次整体搬迁到凤凰山新址。

Archway in Qu Yuan's Hometown

Just like Wen Yiduo, the famous poet and the descendant of the Chu people, once said, "In spirit, there are two kinds of Qu Yuan, one with collectivism of 'serving the king with all loyalty and wisdom'①, the other with individualism of 'getting drowned after showing all talent and personality'②." These two contradictive spirits united in Qu Yuan and formed an idol for later intellectuals③.

Though in *Shi Jing* there are a lot of beautiful and charming poems, they are collective creation without distinctive personal traits. Qu Yuan involved his own dream, experience, sorrow, and adversity into his writing, which made his poetry a milestone with humane warmth and extraordinary personality in Chinese literature.

To commemorate the patriotic poet Qu Yuan, Chinese people have the

① 竭忠尽智，以事其君

② 露才扬己，怨怼沉江

③ 王生铁，《楚文化概要》，湖北人民出版社，2013，p. 150。

Dragon-boat Festival by racing dragon-boat, wrapping Zongzi (pyramid-shaped dumpling filled with glutinous rice, date, or red bean), and so on.

Dragon-boat Festival in Ottawa Canada

The dragon-boat race is a traditional aquatic sports in China. It originated in the ancient Chu State where people raced their boats to save Qu Yuan and

The Logo of the World Dragon Boat Club Crew League of Ottawa, Canada

later made it a custom to race a dragon boat on May 5th of the lunar calendar to commemorate Qu Yuan. Today, the dragon-boat race is not only a way to commemorate Qu Yuan, but also an activity that spreads to Japan, Singapore, Europe and America. The spirit of competition, cooperation and progress conveyed by the Dragon-boat Race has given this sport a long-lasting vitality. The Dragon-boat Race has been included in the national intangible cultural heritage list in China.

9.2 Chu Literature in Song Yu

Sima Qian recorded in *Qu Yuan Jia Sheng Lie Zhuan of The Shiji* like this: "After Qu Yuan died, Song Yu, Tang Le, and Jing Chai were famous for writing odes. Though they learnt to write as Qu Yuan did, they could not admonish bravely as him."① Among them, it is Song Yu who could pass the tradition on.

Song Yu was the student of Qu Yuan and later became the literary courtier of King Qingxiang of Chu. His works included *Jiu Bian* (*Nine Debates*), *Feng Fu* (*Ode to the Wind*), *Shen Nv Fu* (*Ode to the Goddess*), *Gao Tang Fu* (*Ode to Gao Tang*), *Deng Tu Zi Hao Se* (*Prurient Deng Tuzi*), *Dui Chu Wang Wen* (*Answer to Chu King*) and so on. Some famous Chinese allusions such as "Xia Li Ba Ren"②, "Yang Chun Bai Xue"③, and "Qu Gao He Gua"④ came from his works or stories.

---

① 《史记·屈原贾生列传》记："屈原既死之后，楚有宋玉、唐勒、景差之徒者，皆好辞而以赋见称。然皆祖屈原之从容辞令，终莫敢直谏。"

② "下里""巴人"出自《对楚王问》，原指战国时代楚国民间流行的一种歌曲，现比喻通俗的文学艺术。

③ "阳春白雪"代表高雅的文艺作品。

④ 曲高和寡，指的是曲调高深，能跟着唱的人很少。

Song Yu was the beginner to write in odes, which was the source of the odes in the Han Dynasty. As a handsome man in history, Song Yu is used in the idiom of "as handsome as Song Yu or Pan An".

9.3 Chu Literature in Zhuangzi

The essays by Zhuangzi and the poetry by Qu Yuan made the summit of the Chu literature. Zhuang Sao has been referred to the Chu literature①.

Zhuangzi, the essayist and thinker in the Warring States Period, left the world with Zhuangzi, a philosophical and literary book, in which *Xiao Yao You* (*A Happy Excursion*) and *Qi Wu Lun* (*On the Equality of Things*) are the most famous essays full of fascinating allegories and romantic imagination with philosophical thoughts. The exotic imagination made the narration and reasoning persuasive and poetic. The famous scholar Wang Guowei once said, "The imagination of the southern people is much richer and greater than that of the northern people. The southerners are good at analogy, comparison as well as comic. That kind of imagination can never be found in northern literature."②

Zhuangzi was the first Chinese philosopher who proposed to be "sageliness within and kingliness without", that is, "in his inner sageliness, he accomplishes spiritual cultivation; in his kingliness without, he functions in society"③.

The thoughts of Laozi, Zhuangzi, Confucius, and Mengzi constructed the source of Chinese spiritual culture.

---

① 王生铁,《楚文化概要》, 湖北人民出版社, 2013, p. 233。

② 著名学者王国维曾指出:"南人想象力之伟大丰富,胜于北人远甚。彼等长于比类,而善于滑稽……此种想象,决不能于北方文学中发现之。"

③ 冯友兰译注。

参 考 文 献

1. 常俊跃，霍跃红，姚璐，赵永青主编. 中国文化(英文版)[M]. 北京：北京大学出版社，2011.
2. 丛玲玲 编著. 中国漆器[M]. 合肥：黄山书社，2013.
3. 湖北省荆州地区博物馆编. 江陵马山一号楚墓[M]. 北京：文物出版社，1985.
4. 刘芬 编著. 博物馆英语[M]. 天津：天津大学出版社，2018.
5. 李小康 编著. 中国传统漆器[M]. 北京：人民美术出版社，2005.
6. 彭浩 著. 楚人的纺织与服饰[M]. 武汉：湖北教育出版社，1996.
7. 彭林 著. 文物精品与文化中国十五讲[M]. 北京：北京大学出版社，2007.
8. 沈从文 著. 中国古代服饰研究[M]. 上海：上海书店出版社，2011.
9. 谭维四 著. 战国王陵曾侯乙墓[M]. 杭州：浙江文艺出版社，2012.
10. 万全文，院文清 编著. 荆楚文物奇观[M]. 武汉：武汉出版社，2012.
11. 王殿明，杨绮华 编译. 汉英文物考古词汇[M]. 北京：紫禁城出版社，2005.
12. 王生铁 主编. 楚文化概要[M]. 武汉：湖北人民出版社，2013.
13. 叶朗，朱良志 著. 张桂萍 编. 中国文化英语教程[M]. 章思英，陈海燕 译. 北京：外语教学与研究出版社，2010.
14. 张正明 著. 楚史[M]. 武汉：湖北教育出版社，1995.

15. 张正明 著. 楚文化史[M]. 上海: 上海人民出版社, 1987.
16. 张正明 著. 雷电 火焰 凤凰——绘图楚史[M]. 武汉: 湖北少年儿童出版社, 1995.
17. 张正明, 邵学海 主编. 长江流域古代美术: (史前至东汉)绘画与雕刻[M]. 武汉: 湖北教育出版社, 2002.
18. 中国国家博物馆 编. 文物春秋战国史[M]. 北京: 中华书局, 2009.
19. 朱一飞, 佘长茂, 王海燕 编著. 中国文化寓言故事[M]. 唐敦燕, 蔡文谦 译. 上海: 上海外语教育出版社, 2007.
20. Constance A. Cook & Johnson S. Major. *Defining Chu: Image and Reality in Ancient China* [M], Hawaii: University of Hawaii Press, 2004.
21. Gloria K. Fiero. *The Humanistic Tradition: From Prehistory to Medieval Period* [M]. Beijing: Foreign Language and Research Press, 2014.
22. Jessica Harrison-Hall. *China: A History in Objects* [M]. London: Thames & Hudson, the British Museum, 2017.
23. James Legge 译. 道德经(*Tao Te Ching*)[M]. 郑州: 中州古籍出版社, 2016.
24. James Legge 译. 庄子(*The Chuang Tzu*)[M]. 郑州: 中州古籍出版社, 2016.
25. http://www.hbww.org/home/Index.aspx.
26. http://www.jzmsm.org/yk/.
27. http://www.plcsmuseum.com.cn/.
28. http://www.ezbwg.com/.
29. http://www.hnmuseum.com.
30. https://www.dpm.org.cn/Home.html.
31. http://www.ahm.cn.